The Good Girl is Burned Out

and thank f*ck for that

Jo Bolt

© 2024 Jo Bolt

All rights reserved. No portion of this book may be reproduced, stored in a retrieval system, or transmitted in any form or by any means—electronic, mechanical, photocopy, recording, scanning, or other—except for brief quotations in critical reviews or articles, without the prior written permission of the publisher.

Into the Blue Media
hello@intothebluemedia.com

First paperback edition April, 2024

ISBN 978-1-7381833-0-2 (paperback)
ISBN 978-1-7381833-1-9 (e-book)

Cover and Interior Design: Karolina Wudniak, karolinawudniak.com
Cover art: Zoë Pawlak, zoepawlak.com

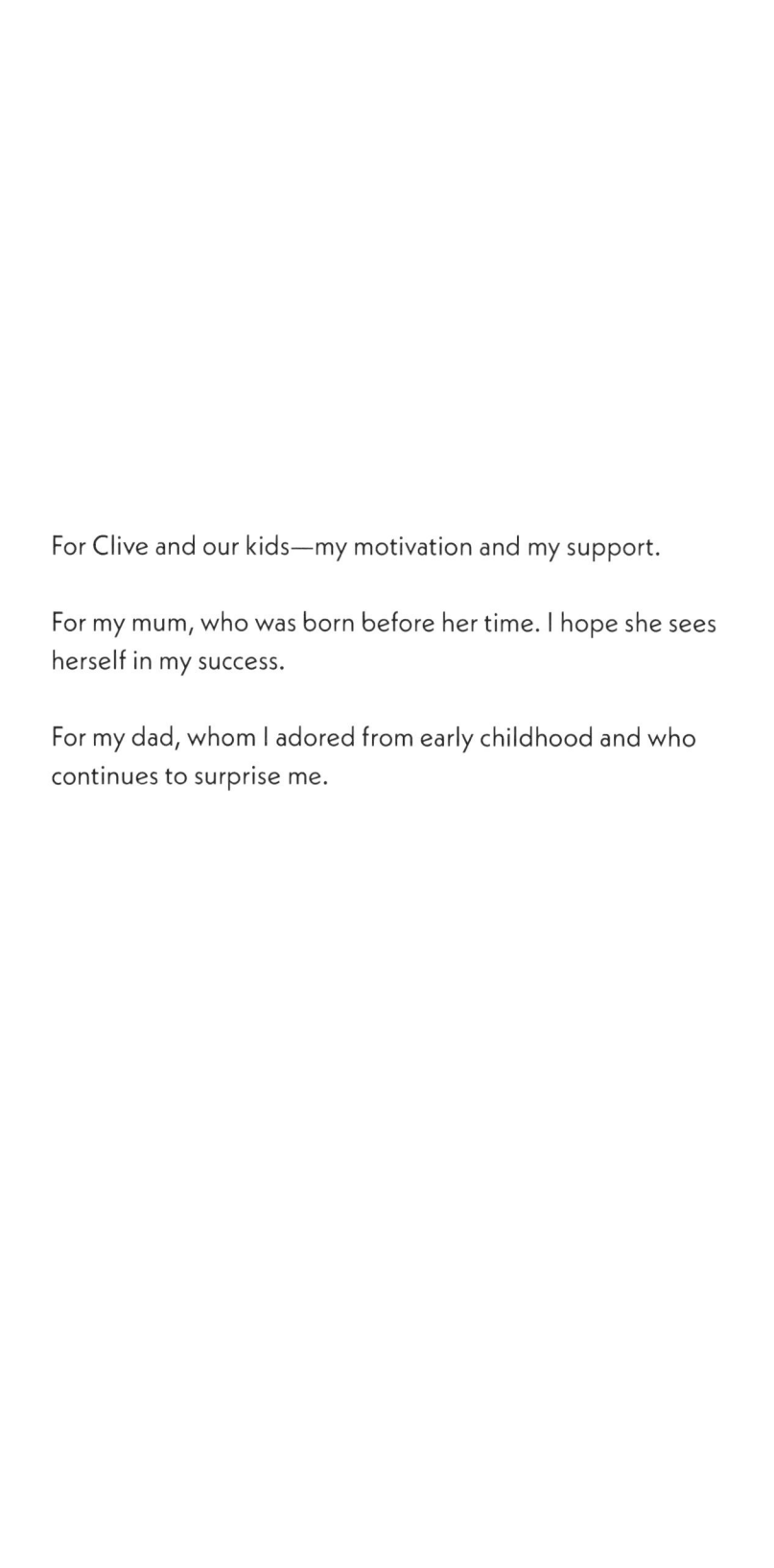

For Clive and our kids—my motivation and my support.

For my mum, who was born before her time. I hope she sees herself in my success.

For my dad, whom I adored from early childhood and who continues to surprise me.

Contents

Note to the Reader	7
Inside Burnout	9
I Can't Breathe	11
The Recipe for Burnout	17
Dawning Realization	23
The Good Girl Origin Story	27
Firstborn	29
Childhood Programming	31
You're Fine	37
Martyr Mindset	41
First Brush with Burnout	43
Sacrifice	47
The Good Girl Grows Up	49
The Cage of Success	51
Gut Punch	55
Manifesting	61
Self-Sabotage	63
I'm Not Good Enough	67
Adding Kids to the Mix	69
Masking Up	73
More than a Manager	75
Worst-Case Scenario	81
The Journey Out of Burnout	85
Stress Leave	87
Tools	89
Meditation	89
Journaling	91
Exercise	94
Therapy & Coaching	97
Community	100
There's Not Enough Time	105

Setting Boundaries	107
Purpose	111
A Kick in the Butt	113
Intentions	115
Pattern Recognition	117
Bad Habits	121
Never Again	125
Writing Again	127
The Journey Continues	129
Family	131
Fear	135
Support & Structure	137
Success	139
Happy Ending	141
The Both/And	143
The Good Girl Community	147
Acknowledgements	149
About the Author	151

Note to the Reader

I wrote this book because I was called to write it.
Ugh. What does that even mean?
Until a few months ago, I would have hard rolled my eyes at that sentence. What the hell does it mean to be called? I would have immediately felt that this book wasn't for me. Perhaps that's how you feel reading it, and believe me, I get it. I was always terrified when people talked about finding your purpose or everyone having a calling. I didn't want to believe in either of them, because I didn't think I had a purpose or a calling.

After twenty-plus years working in the technology industry, climbing the ladder, getting more and more responsibility, earning more, and "succeeding", I burned out. I couldn't sleep, I couldn't take a full breath, I was having panic attacks at the mall, I would flip out at the smallest thing, and I was anxious about everything. So, I took stress leave from work, and started a new journey. Honestly, it was a scarier journey, where I had to deliberately step off the prescribed path and find the one that was more authentically mine. I had to stop judging myself so harshly, and instead turn compassionately towards all the parts of me that were stuck in old stories about not being enough. I had to deliberately reconnect with my body after decades of living in my mind. I had so much I needed to unlearn, and I continue to unlearn it. And that unlearning created space, where I was able to hear the whisper that put me on the path to writing this book. That's what I mean by being called.

I don't think my story is unique. There are generations of women with similar stories of following a prescribed path of who they were told to be—by their families, by society, and ultimately by their own programming. Women who have tamped down their feelings for the comfort of others, who pretzel themselves to fit into what society says is the mould of a good employee, a good daughter, a good sister, a good wife, a good mother, a good friend, a good girl. Women who doubt their value if they're not working harder than everyone else or giving of themselves to other people. If you are one of those women, I hope this book helps you feel seen, and I hope it will help you understand that if I can step off the path, so can you.

With love, Jo

Inside Burnout

I Can't Breathe

The vice-like grip in my chest meant I was physically incapable of taking a full breath. Instead, I would sip air frantically, as if through a straw. Trying desperately to loosen the grip, I turned to doing something physical, as that sometimes worked. That day it was brushing all the debris off the deck with vigorous sweeps of the broom, uplifting music playing as I pushed all my energy into that broom handle, trying to flush away the terror building inside me. But it didn't work. That Sunday afternoon in spring 2021, I couldn't take it anymore. I collapsed in floods of tears on the deck, not knowing what to do with my body to make the feelings go away. I wanted the feelings gone so that I could just live my life.

As I sat sobbing with my husband worriedly bent over me, desperate to find something he could do to stop the pain, my kids appeared at the door. They immediately came and hugged me, not knowing what could be causing Mummy to sob like this, but instinctively comforting me. Then they disappeared, only to reappear as I was shakily trying to explain to my husband what I was feeling. They asked what our favourite colours were, and then disappeared again. It can't have been more than a few minutes later when they both came back, having made me a bracelet out of those little elastics that consisted of four colours—one that represented each of us, me, my husband, and each of them—because they wanted me to have something that would always make me feel better when I looked at it. That was the moment it started to dawn on me that I needed to get help.

I'd been dealing with the physical symptoms of burnout for months. The tightness in my chest and the feeling of not knowing what to do with my body. The constant headaches. The panic attacks that could come on at any time and make me almost pass out if I didn't get my head between my knees. But I carried on, convinced of my own importance in the world and how it meant that I couldn't entertain the idea that there was something seriously wrong, because who would do all the things I did if I weren't able to? Looking back, even the frozen shoulder that I got the year before was likely made worse by the amount of stress I was putting myself under just trying to slog on, even as my body screamed at me to stop.

But all I could think at the time was *what is wrong with me?* Not in a curious, gentle way, but a judgy, frustrated, *what the hell is wrong with me?* kind of way. I had never felt the levels of anxiety I was feeling, snapping at the kids the way that I was, getting irritated at the slightest thing, to the point that my husband felt the need to step between us at times—something he'd never done before. *Why was I worried about everything? Why did everything just seem too much? Why couldn't I cope all of a sudden?* All these questions I asked myself, but certainly not from a place of curiosity. I wanted to get my shit together so that I could get on living my life.

I thought I must be doing something wrong, like I had suddenly forgotten how to do life. I'd forgotten how to be the person with all the answers, the one everyone came to and relied upon. I was angry at myself for feeling this way. Not an ounce of self-compassion did

I have at that moment. I just wanted it to not be true so we could all go back to the way things were supposed to be. I thought about other people who struggled and how I wasn't them. I was the person those people came to for answers. *So why wasn't I showing up like I normally would?*

I had shared some of this with my career/life coach at the time and talked to her about the physical symptoms I was experiencing. I had even expressed concern that the stress I was under could manifest into some kind of physical illness that might impact my ability to be around long-term for my kids. I'd read, for example, that chronic stress can alter the immune system, and that can ultimately result in illness. But I'd admit these fears and then just go back to doing the same things I had been doing previously and ignore my own concerns.

Then, in one session a few weeks after I had shared those concerns, my coach said my words back to me. She said, "Jo, you said you want to be around for your kids in the long term, and I am concerned that if you keep going like this, you might not be able to." That was it. Even though I was the one who had shared that exact concern, hearing it come out of someone else's mouth, the possibility that I might make myself sick and end up not being around for my kids, was too much. That was when I went to my manager and told him that I needed some time off to try and undo the damage I'd already done to myself.

Luckily for me, my manager was a wonderful human and a good friend of mine and he listened to my plan, which was to just take one week off and then return to go through the annual budgeting and planning process, before taking a longer Christmas holiday. He gently suggested that if I felt the way that I described, would it not make more sense to take the extended time off now, rather than wait? I'll always be thankful to him for pushing back on me in that moment. It was definitely the harder option for him and the others on my team, who had to pick up the slack while I was out, but it meant that I could take the time I needed to start the healing process.

At the beginning of my stress leave, I went to my doctor. I described my symptoms and talked about what was going on in my life. She administered a patient health questionnaire and said that my answers indicated that I was suffering from acute anxiety disorder and moderate generalized depression disorder. This came as a shock even though I knew deep down there was something wrong. She talked about lifestyle changes, including meditating and removing stress, and of course, she also started talking about medication.

I'm someone who would rather drink another glass of water than take something for a headache because I want to treat the cause rather than the symptom. So, the idea of taking medication every day was pretty anathema to me. Especially one that affects your body in such a way that you couldn't just stop taking it when you were ready but rather you would need to wean off it.

She was reassuring though, telling me that I would only take a small dose and that sometimes, all the brain needs is the chemicals to interrupt the current pattern for a short period of time to make all the difference, so I wouldn't necessarily need to be on it long term. Still, the idea of being on an antidepressant was very challenging as someone who prides themselves on being "healthy" and not needing drugs. I had a lot of judgement tied up in the idea of taking an antidepressant, even though I was happy such things existed when friends of mine needed them. It just didn't track with who I believed myself to be, as obnoxious as that sounds. It says something about how bad I was feeling, that I decided it was worth a try to add medication to the other things I was doing.

The meds took about a month to properly kick in, but I remember there was a day when I got to the evening and realized that I hadn't had the tightening in my chest for the whole day, which was a first.

Then I added another day to that and then another. I noticed I could be more present with the kids again, and less reactive to their typical kid-like button-pushing behaviour. And wow, did it feel good![1]

---

1   I was on antidepressants for about nine months in total.

The Recipe for Burnout

I'd been running on fumes for months before finally putting my hands up and asking for help.

2021 was a rough year for everyone with the rolling lockdowns courtesy of the pandemic. We'd all expected that somehow the calendar ticking over from 2020 would make things better. I remember thinking that it wouldn't happen immediately, of course, but I was pretty convinced that by spring of 2021 we would be onto better times, whereas in reality, April 2021 saw British Columbia, Canada (where I live) go into yet another lockdown of sorts. At least the kids were in school this time, which helped me as a parent, but it felt like that was done at the cost of all other social interactions.

That year, I was leading the Software Engineering department at a Vancouver-based tech company, and in spring we started to see people quitting in growing numbers. In 2020, everyone had been too worried about what would happen to companies because of the pandemic, so everyone sat tight in their current roles with only a couple of people leaving, which is almost unheard of in the tech industry. But by the time spring 2021 rolled around, the world had changed a bit. People in tech were feeling more confident about the state of our industry, and because of the pandemic, companies in the US were more open to remote work, so they set their sights on Canadian software engineers, wooing them with salaries I just couldn't match. Combine that with people desperate to wrest back control of their lives, which had been taken from them by pandemic protocols, and their jobs became what they could change. So, they quit.

I decided it was all my fault. The old adage says, "People don't leave jobs, they leave their managers," and I was the head of Engineering; ergo, they were leaving me. I remember feeling like I was stumbling from disaster to disaster during this phase, as really key, smart people started leaving. It was like dominoes—the first one leaves and then two others, who weren't originally thinking of leaving, decide to answer one of the frequent pings that they're getting from recruiters on LinkedIn. We were in constant damage mitigation, desperately trying to predict who would be most impacted by the latest departure, both professionally as well as personally, and trying to get ahead of it with our communications.

We were also trying to address what we knew contributed to people's frustrations about working in our Engineering department. During that period, we were getting a lot of feedback from the remaining engineers about what we could be doing better, and the exit interviews were also a trove of great information.

The feedback we were getting gave direction on the areas where we needed to focus, to improve things for those staying. That was the upside. On the downside, it also meant we were getting a lot of negative feedback about everything related to the department—how it was run, how leadership showed up, what we focused on, our processes, and so on. For someone who takes everything to heart, as I was at the time, these exit interviews were rubbing salt into an already open wound. And I wanted to be at the centre of all of it because in my mind, it was all my doing. My inner critic gets really loud when things aren't going well. All the things going wrong around me were evidence that the inner critic would use to lambast me, to remind me that I wasn't good enough because I couldn't even keep my good people. And the answer the inner critic always had for me was that I needed to work harder because hard work was the answer.

I stopped working out because it wasn't a priority. I stopped meditating because who had ten spare minutes a day? I stopped organizing leisure time for myself or with my friends because it was more important to spend alone time working than it was to recuperate or rest. I also started a whole set of new bad habits. I slept less because who had time for eight hours a night when there was so much work to do? I ate more sugar to get the dopamine hit. I offered to help others as a way of feeling worthy, taking time away from my own work to do so, which ratcheted up the stress. I said yes to everything, without even questioning whether I should be doing it because I was so desperate to feel needed and to find something that would "solve" things in the Engineering department.

I would answer work Slack messages, our primary communication mechanism, over breakfast and dinner. I even had my Apple watch set to alert me when a new Slack message came in—the constant buzzing giving me that jolt of panic so no matter what I was doing, I was dragged back into thinking about work. I was also consistently opening my laptop as soon as the kids were in bed and looking at work right through to bed at 11 p.m., where I'd stare at the ceiling while my mind whirred.

On top of that, I'd often ask my husband to take the kids for a few hours on a Sunday because I needed to 'prep for the week' to go into Monday without the crushing fear that I was already feeling each Sunday afternoon. I barely saw my kids and didn't talk to my husband, even though we were both working from home full-time. I was so consumed by what was going on at work that I didn't have the energy for anything else. What brief time I did take away from work at the weekend was to fill my cup to better pour from it solidly for the whole of the next workweek.

Looking back, I wasn't even doing great work in those evenings and in those hours that I worked at the weekend. Often, I was doing busywork because I was too exhausted to do the real work, but I couldn't allow myself to rest in the state I was in. It sounds utterly ludicrous as I look back now, but I was caught up in the story, not only of being the one who was responsible for the mess but also the saviour who was required to get everyone out of the mess.

I had this interesting duality going on in my head at this time, and to be honest, it was just an amplification of a story that I'd been telling myself forever. On the one hand, I thought that I wasn't good enough, that someone else would not have got the team into this situation, that someone else would be able to handle this better, that someone else would be able to solve things more gracefully and effectively than I could. And on the other hand, I would not ask for help. Asking for help meant I didn't have the answer, and it was very important to my good girl identity that others believed I had the answer and knew what I was doing. This is quite literally the opposite of what I would talk to my team about—I expected them to come to me when things were hard and they needed help, and I was very vocal if they chose to try and muscle through something themselves and made it worse. But somehow, I did not think that this applied to me.

I've come to learn that many of the ingredients that contributed to my personal burnout recipe started with my good girl identity. But it was only the addition of the 'not good enough' story that then made the concoction so potent as to cause my physical and emotional burnout.

As part of the "not good enough" story, I'd go to all meetings that I was invited to, even if they didn't have an agenda or were suddenly scheduled right in the middle of some focus time that I had created to get a specific thing done. I'd add to my workload regularly by being the first to put their hand up in the meeting if a task needed doing, even if I wasn't the logical person to do it. I had such fear of getting left behind or being passed over for the next opportunity that I had no boundaries in terms of when I'd say yes.

This story impacted how I showed up as a manager as well. If the people who reported to me didn't follow through on something they had said they'd do, I wouldn't help them hold themselves accountable, because I could always see some failing in my own guidance or expectation setting that might explain why they hadn't completed the task. Often, I'd choose to take it on myself, rather than have a conversation with them about what had got in the way of them doing it. This piled onto my own workload, while also robbing my team of the opportunity to grow.

Dawning Realization

I sought career/life coaching at the beginning of 2021 because I knew I wanted to be doing something different with my life. I didn't know what it was, but I felt something else was out there for me. I didn't realize then that while I wanted help moving forward, I was stuck in a deep rut that I'd been digging myself into for a long time. I remember turning up to coaching so many times, already feeling like a failure because I hadn't prepared anything to talk about because I was always "doing." I was always "so busy." My coaching sessions felt like evidence of exactly how I did not have my shit together. I mean, if I couldn't even get it together to prepare for coaching, which I was paying for out of my own pocket, how would I get it together in the rest of my life?

And then my coach would do her job, and she would ask me big questions and challenge me to look at things differently. She never gave me answers, because that wasn't her role, but God how I wanted someone to give me answers. I remember telling her at the time that I felt like a hamster on a wheel slowly sinking below the surface of the water, frantically running, always running, but sinking, nonetheless.

There's a frustration that comes when people tell you a suite of tools that you can use to help you get out of whatever rut you're stuck in, but they can't tell you the specific way that you should use the tools. They'll say things like, "It's different for everybody" or "What works for me might not work for you" or "You've just got to listen to yourself and work it out."

When you've been living in the logical side of your mind your whole life, like I have, there is no sense of what your body is telling you or what might be right for you in the moment, because you can't rationalize that. You have to feel it, and feeling it is like a muscle that for me, had atrophied over my whole life. It was like a bicep that couldn't even lift a cup of coffee. I wanted so hard to hear what my body was telling me, what was right for me, but I'd got so used to ignoring it, that when I wanted to hear it, I couldn't.

I was so frustrated. I felt like it was a cop-out on the part of the people saying there was no right way. It felt like an abandonment of their responsibilities to me because they weren't guiding me like I wanted to be guided. I wanted to know what the answer was. What the right answer was. Because there had to be one. But instead, all they gave me was more questions.

There was one particular session when my coach was trying to help me get out of my rut and challenge me to think about the future and she asked me a big, open question, and my response was anger. I felt this ball of rage immediately form inside of me and it burst up through my chest and out of my throat in the form of "How the hell am I supposed to be able to answer something like that when I can barely even make it through a regular day?" To her credit, she was so calm in the face of my desperation. I don't recall what she said, but I think that might have been the start of the realization, for both of us, that coaching wasn't really helping in that moment—I simply wasn't capable of thinking about the future because the present was so overwhelming.

I started wondering about therapy. As someone who grew up in England, this wasn't a natural step for me. Growing up, we derided Americans' desperate need to tell strangers their problems. We saw it as weak and self-indulgent, and we would roll our eyes when it came up in a TV show or something we read. It just wasn't done. We had the mental fortitude to solve our own problems. We believed we were stronger (and inherently better) than them because we could do this ourselves.

That said, I'd been living on the west coast of Canada long enough that I'd softened somewhat to the idea of therapy, and in fact, my husband and I had been to couples therapy a few times and it had really helped us, so it wasn't a completely alien idea. When my coach suggested gently to me that perhaps I would be better served looking into my past with therapy and understanding what was underneath the pain I was clearly in, rather than keep trying to look into the future with coaching, I decided she was right. Luckily, my coach is a connector with a wonderful network of humans with incredible skills in all areas. She sent me a list of three possible therapists who she thought would be a match for me, and I only needed to get a couple of lines into the bio of the first one before I knew I had my person.

During the first session I had with my therapist, I came right out and said that I was sceptical of what therapy could do for me. I have a great relationship with my parents, so I had no desire to spend a bunch of time talking to someone who was going to help me understand that it was somehow their fault that I am the way I am. She assured me that while we were going to do some excavating of my childhood, it was for the purpose of learning and understanding what had happened to me, and how I had responded to things that had happened to me. It would do nobody any good to assign blame because then we get into the victim mindset where we are not the masters of our own destiny, and then we're not able to make the change we need to live in a different way.

So, that's where I started to go back and understand the origin story of the person I was then (because I'm an evolution of her now). I began to understand how I got there and what I might need to do, understand, forgive, and reprogram in order to not only get myself out of the physical and mental burnout I was in but also learn how to not get back there again and live differently moving forward.

The Good Girl Origin Story

Firstborn

I was born in England, near Birmingham—my parents' first child and the first grandchild to be born on my dad's side of the family. My dad's family lived close to us, and as a result, I was surrounded by doting adults, whose attention I didn't have to share for a solid two years until my brother came along. The early stories of me are of a precocious child who was stringing complex sentences together from a young age and delighting the grown-ups around her.

I learned early how to please the adults around me. I understood that they loved well-behaved kids, who don't have big emotions, who say and do the "right" things. When my brother was born, in fact, my mum tells of how, at not quite two years old, I went and gathered nurses in the ward to come and marvel at the wonder of the new baby. You can imagine the delight that this brought to not only my parents but the nurses as well.

There are other stories that my parents tell of Saturday mornings when we would go for breakfast at the local department store cafe, and rather than sitting with our parents and eating our toast and teacakes, we'd wander off and engage in conversation with a table of old ladies who were having tea.[2]

---
2   A teacake is very similar to a hot cross bun.

As a parent now myself, I know how it feels when your kid engages well with other adults, and I remember rushing to congratulate that behaviour in my own kids and feeling that it meant that I'd done something right as a parent. Their "good" behaviour feels like a reflection on us and it's pretty intoxicating. Much of parenting is not knowing what the hell you're doing and making it up on the fly, so getting positive feedback from other adults feels great. As a kid, my ability and willingness to interact in such an adult manner at an early age was met with smiles and praise, so very early on I learned that this behaviour was rewarded and resulted in greater connection with my parents and other adults, and so I leaned into that way of being.

My brother did not learn those same things. Or, more accurately, knowing him, he understood them, but it didn't suit him to be so contained. My recollection of being his elder sibling is of wanting to manage his chaos, smooth over the rough patches, and make everything calm. This is not to say that my brother was anything other than a normal kid, challenging boundaries, testing rules, and learning what worked and what didn't. That's exactly what he was. He was doing his job as a kid. The challenge was not in his behaviour, but rather in my response to it.

Childhood Programming

I had an early ingrained fear of chaos and unpredictability, which likely came in part as my response to how my parents handled their anger. My mum had a pretty volcanic temper when she was pushed hard enough, which is a talent that children have. She was our primary caregiver as my dad worked away from home Monday to Friday from when I was about six, so she was solely responsible for my brother and me.

She could handle a lot, and not only did she do the regular childcare, but she also found time to hand-create clothing for us, do endless crafts, make dress-up costumes, and bake spectacular birthday cakes. I still remember a Hungry Caterpillar birthday cake that she made for my brother's second birthday. She gave us a huge amount of herself, and understandably, sometimes it all got a bit much; we'd push her buttons and she'd explode, yelling at us and maybe we'd get the occasional smacked bottom, which, though I realize I'm dating myself, wasn't an unusual thing when I was growing up.

Dad also had a temper, but he was afraid of it and what it would do to us if it were unleashed. I recall my mum saying that she couldn't argue with my dad because he would say hurtful things that he'd forget as soon as the argument was over, but that she couldn't forget. And he knew this, so he handled it in the only way he knew how—he would go silent. Many different things could trigger a bout of silence from my dad—we kids could misbehave, something could have happened at work, or England could have lost a key rugby game. You didn't know when the silence might start or what might trigger it, and when it did happen, you didn't know how long it would last. The not knowing was something that I then tried to control by being as good a girl as I possibly could be. I became hyperaware of situations that might rock the boat, and my brother's typical child behaviour became a threat to the calm, so my response was to try even harder to control the things that I could control because he was (to my mind) so unpredictable.

I understand now, from reading about attachment theory, that the scariest thing for a child is losing attachment with the key caregivers in their life, which are often their parents.[3] As children, we completely depend on those key caregivers for survival. We learn quickly what behaviours sever that attachment and we learn what behaviours strengthen that attachment. The angry outbursts from my mum were one way that the attachment would be severed, but the scariest thing for me as a child was not those moments, because they were short-lived and somewhat predictable; it was the periods of silence from my dad, because in those cases, they could come out of nowhere, and I had no idea how long they were going to last.

And so came the hypervigilance, which has been both my superpower and my Achilles heel in my personal life and my career. On the superpower side, it means I can read people and situations in a way that others can't. I can see in someone's body language that something is going on, or in the dynamics of a meeting, where we need to focus our attention to help a team work better together. More than once, I've made an observation to a colleague about

---

3   I found Dr Becky Kennedy's book *Good Inside* a great starting point for understanding attachment theory.

why they've said or done something, and they've responded, "How could you possibly know that?"

This has helped me immensely in my career and has made me an empathetic leader. And I say "empathetic" rather than "compassionate" because the downside of this acutely attuned hypervigilance is that I take on the emotion and often the heaviness that an individual or a team are feeling, and eventually it can become debilitating for me.

The other downside of hypervigilance is that it means I'm never just having the conversation that I'm having. I'm constantly mapping out possible outcomes of a situation and trying to work out how I can make everything work or make things better and solve the problem. It can mean I'm distracted, and even when I've made a decision, I worry about whether it's the right one. While your average person would have moved on from something, I'm still revisiting my decisions and wondering whether I could have done better.

Another place the "good girl" persona really showed up was in school. Other than being told that I talked too much in class early in my school days, I always had exceptional report cards. I was usually the kid who listened and understood the assignment. I always did my homework without being asked. I got good grades. I got into a private secondary school.[4] I got one detention in my whole school career and unbelievably that was actually a case of mistaken identity. I was probably about thirteen and sitting with other girls who had arrived at school too late for our morning assembly because our school bus had been caught in traffic. When this happened, the rule was that you had to wait in a room next to the main assembly hall that was only separated by concertina doors that were not soundproof, so you had to sit in silence. Some girls next to me were not doing as they had been asked, and so the teacher in charge of our waiting group

---

4 Secondary school is the English equivalent of high school.

handed out detentions for talking, and I got caught up in the punishment because of my proximity to the group. The hilarious thing about this is that I was such a "good girl" that I couldn't even take the lunchtime detention that had been handed out because I had orchestra practice, so I ended up in a significantly shorter detention.

Later in life, I remember watching an episode of the TV show *Frasier*, which is about brothers who are both psychiatrists, one of whom (the titular character Frasier) has his father living with him. There is a scene where Frasier and his dad, Martin, a retired cop who is incredibly down to earth and somewhat perplexed by having two rather pretentious, fancy sons, are reminiscing and laughing about an episode where young Frasier had eaten pot brownies and streaked at a football game. Niles, the younger son, begs Martin to tell a story about what he got up to as a kid and Martin just claps a hand on Niles' shoulder and says, "Niles, there aren't any stories, you were just a good kid". In that moment, my stomach dropped, and my jaw hit the floor because I realized that I was Niles. There weren't stories of high jinks and testing boundaries because I just hadn't done it. I'd been so focused on being good.

With my lack of getting into trouble and my consistent attention in class, being clever became part of my good girl identity. We weren't taught about having a growth mindset, and my school was very focused on grades because that's what helped it in the rankings of private schools, and it's what attracted new families to want to pay for their children to go there. Grade A's were rewarded and all teaching was done with the focus on getting as good grades as possible in our GCSE and then A level exams.[5] It became a story in our extended family and with my parents' friends—Jo is clever—and I bought into it wholeheartedly because it felt good.

---

5 GCSE is the standard exam taken at sixteen years old in England, and A levels are taken at eighteen.

You learn very quickly what behaviour is rewarded in the system in which you're operating. I've seen this in companies throughout my career. You can have a statement about the culture you're building and who you are as a company, but if that's at odds with the behaviours you reward or the actions your leadership takes, then it's not that culture that takes hold; it's the underlying one that is fed by those behaviours and actions. I was in a system that rewarded obedience and good grades, so I learned to live within the system, and I excelled at it. We weren't encouraged to think differently or creatively, but to answer the questions on the tests in the way that would allow us to get good grades.

In contrast, my brother didn't enjoy school. In his teens, he ended up in a weekly boarding situation whereby he stayed at school from Monday to Friday and only came home for the weekends. Because he didn't enjoy classroom learning and was likely bored, he would get into trouble, and I recall my parents having to go to the school on multiple occasions. It's unlikely that it was anything out of the norm, but because it was juxtaposed with the way that I went through school, there were unfair comparisons made, with my way of being considered more "right" by the wider family.

When I think about it now, having my own children, and witnessing what school is like for them, I think that trying to get kids to sit still for long periods of time from a young age, and learn things by rote, is such a broken system. My brother is smart and therefore bored easily, and boredom often breeds behaviour described as "acting out." Through my lens of hypervigilance, I saw these episodes and noted the stress that it brought my parents and the disconnection between them and my brother when they would happen, and it further reinforced my need to be "good" and to not rock the boat.

I wasn't a natural in school. I had to work at it. I recall when I first encountered algebra; I railed at the introduction of letters into equations. *Why on earth would there be letters where there should be numbers?* It made no sense to me. I remember my mum very patiently explaining that it was because sometimes you didn't know what the number would be and my response was "Well, why can't you just guess?" and she patiently asked me how I would guess if it was 3.67849.

I had similar challenges when I started to learn Spanish—I was told that to say, "I go" which would be "je vais" in French, was just "voy" in Spanish and not "yo voy" because the person doing the going was inherent in the word "voy." You didn't need the Spanish word for "I" (yo). I was so frustrated and confused by this because it didn't match the framework that I understood for language. And don't get me started on German and the way that they sometimes stack the verbs at the end of the sentence!

All this to say, new concepts were hard for me, but being the diligent student that I was, I worked through them. Luckily for me, I had my mum (who had done double maths A level) and a wonderful maths teacher called Mrs Kent, who could explain the same idea in three different ways, one of which would finally resonate with my brain. Working hard was something that I understood I had to do if I was going to be the person that everyone said I was—the high achiever, the grade A student. And that was incredibly important to me because that's who I had already internalized that I was.

You're Fine

Growing up in England, as a child of the eighties, was definitely a different experience to being a kid today. I was not growing up in the *children should be seen and not heard* era, at least not in my family. However, there was still an understanding that you should always respect your elders. When it came to discipline, my mum recently told me that while she and dad tried not to squash our personalities, they believed that they should discipline me and my brother so that we would behave acceptably for others. Amongst other things, this meant that having big feelings, especially in public, wasn't acceptable.

I took this at face value when she told me, as her reasoning resonated with my desire to never put other people out or make them uncomfortable. But sitting with it longer, I realized that while the original motivation might have felt like it was for other people, I think deep down it was likely my parents' fear of experiencing their own feelings. Growing up in the era they did, with the *stiff upper lip* English culture, they had no reference point for people feeling so-called negative emotions in a healthy way. Their parents hadn't modelled this for them, so they didn't have the tools to do it for themselves or for their kids. Nor did they understand why it wasn't healthy to stuff their feelings down, because they didn't have access to all the information that we do today.

I recently saw a comedian talking about how our generation of parents has really got the short end of the stick. When we were young and we had big feelings, we were told they weren't appropriate, or that we were fine, because our parents didn't know how to handle our emotions. Now we're parenting our own kids in an age when we're encouraged to pay attention to and validate all of our children's feelings, including the incandescent rage that they feel when you won't let them eat the gum they just found stuck to the coffee shop table.

It's not easy to do when you haven't been shown how. Say one of my children has fallen out with their friend on the playground and is now howling at the top of their lungs about being left out. I want them to be OK, and I also really want them to stop screaming because it's drawing attention, which I find uncomfortable, and it might be bothering other people, so I approach them and say, "You're fine. You're OK." For me, it's still an instinctive reaction because that's what I was told as a child, and because I was taught to think about how my actions, which now extend to my children's actions, would impact other people. It's a response that means well because I really do want my child to be fine, but what it actually tells them is that they can't trust their own feelings. They don't feel fine in the moment, but their mum is telling them that they are fine, and they trust me to know more than them, so they stop believing themselves.

I have first-hand experience of what happens when you stop believing your own feelings or ignore your gut. For example, there have been a few occasions in my career when I've been charged with hiring a new team member, and I've known that it's not a good idea to hire a particular candidate. I couldn't explain why at the time and because everyone else on the hiring committee was a yes, we've gone ahead and hired them, against my gut feeling. Nine times out of ten, it hasn't worked out. In those instances, I had the authority to veto the hire and I didn't do it, because I didn't trust my intuition. I had no explicit data to back up my feelings and was taught that my feelings couldn't be trusted, so I trusted what other people thought instead.

    These days I notice when I'm doing the "You're fine" thing with my own children because I have a better understanding of the consequences, and I can quickly correct myself in the moment and switch to "Are you ok?" instead. It's a small change, but it gives authority for their feelings back to my child and builds their trust in themselves. A trust I am only just rebuilding for myself.

Martyr Mindset

When I was born, my mum gave up work as a computer programmer and didn't go back until I was ten. There were a couple of motivators for her returning to work, the first being that she and my dad had decided that we would go to private secondary school. The other reason was that she was tired of us all taking her for granted.

Sadly, her going back to work didn't really change us taking her for granted. Looking back, I'm reminded of the amount of time she still spent looking after our household after she got home from her full-time job. I remember sitting in the lounge, watching TV or reading, and being distinctly put out when she would call from the kitchen and ask me to lay the table after slaving away on her own, creating a delicious, nutritious meal for us all.

Mum did all the heavy lifting regarding anything to do with running the house or ensuring that we kids had what we needed for school. She also planned all our holidays and kept the social calendar. And then she'd do things like hosting a Christmas Eve party for thirty-plus people with full meal options and multiple desserts, before then hosting a full Christmas Day dinner that she got up early to prepare. And before that, she would have bought everyone's gifts and spent any "spare" time in the run-up to Christmas baking and decorating the Christmas cake and hand-making truffles and petits fours so that we had festive homemade treats to put out when people came over. I grew up thinking this level of self-sacrifice on the part of women, with no help from your family, was normal.

Mum was also the one who encouraged me to do everything. She didn't go to university herself and instead got a job straight after school at eighteen, but she wanted me to go. When the opportunity came up for me to do a gap year in South America between school and university, she was the one who championed me in investigating the options, completing the application, and attending the briefings. I honestly don't believe I would have gone if it weren't for her support, and it was an experience that fundamentally changed me.

Even though Mum would still only have been in her forties then, a similar age to me now, there was a sense that certain doors were now closed to her and so she would live vicariously through me. And of course, Mum had learned from her mum and so on. Both my grandmas were in awe that I was going solo to South America, and they avidly followed my progress via a world encyclopaedia each and long phone conversations with my mum, where she'd help them locate where I was through instructions like "You remember she was in Asunción? Well, go three inches to the right, to the other side of Paraguay, and you'll find Iguazu Falls. That's where she is now." We still have the encyclopaedias with the Post-it notes that they wrote.

It's hard for me to imagine believing that my own story is largely written at this age. I feel like I'm just beginning. For my mum though, the fact that she was out working was new for her generation, as my grandma had stayed at home. Mum was breaking generational patterns herself in many ways, and giving me a new baseline to start from, but there's only so much one generation can do.

First Brush with Burnout

Shortly after I got back from my trip to South America and was at university, I had my first brush with burnout, though at the time, I had no idea that's what it was, and it wasn't happening to me; it was happening to my mum.

She was working as a computer programmer, as the team and project lead, and she had been in her role for several years, but she hit a wall. She could no longer accept the dissonance between the company mission statement and the behaviours she was seeing, but she had no idea what else she could do. She talked to the people at work and organized to take six weeks off to assess the situation. Talking to her about this later, she told me that it didn't occur to her to look for a different career in a different company to find something that fulfilled her. This was back in the nineties before everything was on the internet, so it was much harder to find information about what was available, and it was very much frowned upon to job hop because it was still a work environment where people had jobs for life.

I remember my own reaction to this period in Mum's life. I wasn't directly impacted as I was off at university, living my own life, but I distinctly recall hearing what was happening and wondering when

Mum was just going to pull it together and get back to work. It didn't occur to me that she was being true to herself and listening to her body, because I didn't understand those concepts at all. What I knew was that my mum was doing something I'd never heard of anyone doing before, and I just wanted her to get back to "normal" and be like the other mums.

She was also getting involved with life coaching and reiki, which were very foreign concepts to me at the time. They felt fluffy and insubstantial then, though I've personally relied on a great deal of coaching in recent years. Reiki, in particular, brought me real anxiety because Mum would talk about the fact that she got a very distinct energetic impact when she did reiki on me compared to anyone else, but as the recipient of the reiki, I just couldn't feel anything. She talked about "sending me reiki" before she would go to sleep at night and I would smile and say thanks, not believing you could do such a thing.

As someone who wanted everything to make sense and be predictable so that it could be managed, I was thrown by Mum's change in behaviour, and I saw my dad as the safe space. He could be relied upon to stay steady, as it took a great deal to change his mind about things. A lot of my early opinions were informed by what my dad thought, rather than my mum, which seems so unfair given that she was the one who took primary care of us. It was doubtless partly due to his absence because he was working away, and partly due to the bouts of silence. I was always looking for ways to connect with him when we were together, and having the same opinion about something was a great way of connecting. I didn't have to try with Mum, because she was always around and emotionally available to us, so it was safe for us to disagree.

Mum has commented that she felt like an outsider within our family of four because my brother and I share my dad's sarcastic sense of humour, and back then we also shared his opinions on many subjects. I think about the phrase "Familiarity breeds contempt" and how true it seems in this case, where we so took her love for granted that we would collectively roll our eyes when she challenged our scornful view on certain things; for example, when she questioned why we all had to band together to hate whatever team England was playing rugby against, rather than just enjoy the game.

When I was going through my own burnout, I remember my mum saying that she wished she had handled things as well as I was. But the fact is, there was no way she could have, because everything was stacked against her. I think about how different things would have been for me if I'd experienced this in the nineties, like her, when there weren't the support structures that exist today and even your own family didn't understand what you were going through. Getting therapy was unheard of, and I doubt she could even talk to her friends about what she was feeling as it wasn't "done" to be struggling. Burnout wasn't a term that was used, so she couldn't look around and see herself in any literature or understand that she wasn't the only one going through this.

And so, after six weeks, she just went back to work because that was what you did. And while it pains me to admit it, knowing what I know now, at the time I breathed a sigh of relief because Mum was "back."

Sacrifice

When I was in my mid-teens, my dad gave up working as a self-employed management consultant and took a job as a quality manager at a parcel company. The consulting work had meant he travelled a lot and was often gone during the week, and by nature of it being consulting, the engagements were for a few months at a time and not as predictable as he felt they needed to be, given that my parents had decided to send us to paid private school. From what I recall and from conversations with him since, he really enjoyed the consulting work. He liked helping clients, and he liked solving their problems.

The quality manager role had none of the things that he liked about the work he'd done before, but it did mean that he was home, and his income was more predictable. I don't think he talked to me directly about not being happy in his job, but I knew that he didn't like it. I knew that he preferred the work he'd been doing before, and I knew that he'd made this decision so that my brother and I could have the life he and Mum wanted for us.

I internalized that fact, and I understood from his decision, and from the way that my mum sacrificed herself for us, that self-sacrifice was what you did for the people you loved. You put them first. You didn't prioritize what you wanted because you had a responsibility to others. I understood that selflessness was an admirable trait. I understood this both from looking at my own family, but also from being a girl and then a woman in the world, where we are constantly delivered the message that this is how we should be—we should aim to be selfless, which is essentially to have a lack of self. We've had generations of (mainly) women who have been taught that not having a self is the highest form of being, that you've really succeeded if you can point at how much you have given up of your own desires and needs and put others first.

This is quite different to being of service to others. I do believe that we have a responsibility to be of service to others, to lift them up and help those less fortunate than us, and of course, I want to do things for my family. But I now believe we need to do that from a place of empowerment and self-fulfilment. I believe we can be most of service to others if we have a full self. We need to know who we are, how to name our needs, and how to ask for what we need and fill our own cups so that we can give to others. You don't need to give up your whole self to be of service. In fact, you can do more for others when you are your own fulfilled self.

The Good Girl Grows Up

The Cage of Success

When I finished university in the early 2000s, I moved to London, along with pretty much everyone I knew, and got a job at PricewaterhouseCoopers (PwC) as an IT consultant. I did well at PwC and then at IBM, but I didn't like the work, so when my boyfriend at the time (now my husband) asked whether I'd like to move to Vancouver with him, I said yes.

We moved to Vancouver in 2005, and my first job when I arrived was with a software company. There I grew from project manager for the Systems and Infrastructure team to taking on some additional software teams to program manager. I brought my Protestant work ethic to the role, taking on more and more responsibility and working longer hours than were prescribed. I recall a couple of major projects where, for a few months at a time, I was working from 8 a.m. to 8 p.m. every day and thinking about work over the weekend. But I felt important. I was at the heart of everything, and I didn't have kids, so my time was my own to give, and I gave it gladly.

From that role, I went on to lead a custom development team at another software company, and as I proved myself capable of handling whatever got thrown at me, my scope grew and grew. I thrived in this environment. I loved being at the centre of everything.

I loved the thrill of being asked to take on something new because it meant I was succeeding, and I never got bored.

Nothing at all seemed wrong with the trajectory I was on because I was climbing the ladder in terms of responsibility, my salary was going up, and I was getting shit done. I garnered such a reputation for delivering that if there was an issue that senior people didn't know how to approach when it came to technology, I was often drafted in to help them understand it because I spoke both their language and the language of the technical teams.

Upon returning from my second maternity leave, I was asked to manage a mission-critical technology migration project that involved taking millions of rows of data from our existing platform and migrating them to a completely new platform with different functionality and structure. This meant managing a team of eighty-plus people across two continents and delivering the project in a way that had practically no downtime for the business.

I had two very young kids at this point, but I adapted my work hours so that three days a week I'd be in the office by 7 a.m. so that I could work with the team in the UK. At the time it felt like a necessary step to keep my career on its upward trajectory, and my husband and I made it work, but it started to take its toll on us.

Looking back, I don't regret climbing the ladder. I thrived on challenge; I loved learning new things, and my work ethic and delivery mindset meant that I was given a lot of opportunity to grow. What I do see though is a lot of evidence in my decisions of my lack of trust in myself and my fear of disappointing people, which made me pretzel myself into unnatural shapes and work even harder when things got tough. In my twenties and early thirties, the impact of this behaviour was masked by the abundance of time available to me. I didn't have any real commitments, so I could feed my need to prove myself through hours committed to work.

By the time I was managing the migration project, I was starting to struggle, but I thought it was environmental in nature—that it was the work, or the company, or the number of demands on my time—and that if I could change some of those, things would be fine. I didn't understand yet that different parts of me were in conflict with each other. I didn't understand that a part of me was railing against my lack of boundaries and willingness to say no to myself to please others, or that there was a part of me that wanted me to acknowledge that I couldn't and shouldn't be responsible for everything. And that those parts were in conflict with the parts of me that wanted to keep me "safe" and small—the cautionary parts that were founded in early stories of my value being tied to my goodness, which meant I needed to keep working hard, going above and beyond, and putting other people's needs ahead of my own.

So, I just kept working at it and pushing along because I had yet another story within myself about quitting—it just wasn't something I could entertain. Quitting was failure, and admitting failure would be devastating to me because it threatened the core of who I believed myself to be. Good girls were reliable and they powered through the hard stuff. They didn't complain and they didn't quit.

Gut Punch

As the project wound to a close, the team and I were on a high—we'd had a really successful launch and had increased the valuation of the business through our endeavours. I started to wonder about what was next. I knew I didn't enjoy being part of the leadership team at the company because I felt there wasn't an environment of trust, and I didn't feel respected or valued. But then we started talking about me becoming the chief product officer (CPO). You'd think the last thing I'd want to do would be to take a high-level executive position in a company where I didn't feel valued, but I talked myself into this being a good opportunity. I could try this stretch role in an environment I understood and then use the experience to pivot to a new company.

Hindsight obviously tells me that I was lying to myself. I knew it wasn't really much of an opportunity. I knew that it was going to be challenging, and it meant that I was going to intentionally be putting myself into the thick of this environment that was unhealthy for me, but I was afraid of not taking it. I was afraid that it was the best I could do and if I didn't take it, I may never get offered a similar role elsewhere. So, I negotiated a great salary for myself and laid out the key points of the role. The documents came through for me to sign along with an email from the CEO. I don't remember the details of that email, but I do remember understanding immediately that we had different expectations of what a CPO would do. I paused. I was about to go on holiday for three weeks to catch up with friends and family in Europe, so I asked that we hold off on signing until I returned so that we could ensure that we were completely on the same page about what the role would involve. And off I went on holiday.

Upon my return, I had a regularly scheduled one-to-one phone call with the CEO during which I anticipated talking about the job description and clarifying everything. He seemed uncomfortable when we first got on the call and asked whether our Human Resources (HR) person was there. She was flying in from Toronto that day ostensibly to spend some time with the Vancouver team, so I merrily told him she hadn't arrived at the office yet. To which he responded, "Well, she's supposed to be at this meeting."

Still clueless about what was happening, I saw her turn up at the office door and greeted her with a big hug, letting her know that I was having a meeting that she was supposed to be in and ushering her into the conference room. She was somewhat flustered, but that still didn't register as anything to be concerned about for me. I let the CEO know that she was now here, and we could get started. It still wasn't until he said, "So, Joanne…" that the penny finally dropped that I was being let go.

Other than saying out loud, "Oh shit, I'm being fired," I was practically mute on the call. I was in shock, as I hadn't seen it coming at all. I had just successfully delivered a massive project that had increased the valuation of the company and we'd been *this close* to signing a new job offer for the CPO role, and now suddenly I didn't have any job. And while it's true that I hadn't been happy and had considered that being let go would be a good thing, when it actually happened, I had a real *how dare you dump me, I was going to dump you!* Moment.

It was the first time in my career that I had been let go, and I understand that I was fortunate for that to be my first experience. But as a result of making it so far without the experience, I'd made up stories that this wasn't the kind of thing that happened to me. It happened to other people. And while I would tell those other people that it was no reflection on them, I secretly believed it was because I wasn't one of those people.

The first few weeks after being laid off were rough. My ego was dented in a significant way. I couldn't believe this had happened to me. And even as I tell the story all these years later, I recognize that I have a need to show how bizarre the circumstances were around being laid off so that others understand that it was through no fault of my own that it happened. I notice that I do a similar thing when I talk about being part of a round of layoffs at another company, which happened a few years later. The story that I tell there centres around actively wanting to be laid off. And that's not inaccurate at all, but the way I tell the stories to others is interesting, as I clearly still have some internalized judgement related to being laid off that I haven't yet let go of.

I have a complicated relationship with my career. The first layoff helped me realize how much of who I believed myself to be was wrapped up in my job. I sourced the majority of my value from the validation I got in my work. Managing people, leading large initiatives, being asked for my opinion, leveraging my experience, solving challenging problems—they all happened at work, and they very much defined me.

I think it took me a good six weeks for the ego bruise of the layoff to fade. Six weeks where I couldn't allow myself to enjoy the privilege of time to work out what I wanted to do and to find a job. Six weeks of coming to terms with the fact that I am someone who gets laid off and that this doesn't just happen to specific types of other people. This probably seems ridiculous because there have been so many layoffs in the technology industry in recent history that it's going to be rare to find someone who doesn't have first-hand experience with it, but the first time it happened to me there was nothing going on in the sector and there were no "rounds" of layoffs occurring. It was a very targeted laying off of one person—me.

As I no longer had a job, I was going to more technology industry meet-ups to understand what roles were out there and what I might want to do. At these events, I would meet new people and the first thing they would ask me was "What do you do?" I experimented with how to answer this question, and I honestly never found a way that felt authentic to me and made for a smooth conversation with a new person. Initially, I tried to be completely honest and let them know that I was currently unemployed and trying to decide what I wanted to do next, but that led to most folks realizing that I wasn't of immediate use to them and the conversation very quickly petering out. The next thing I tried was telling them something like, "I solve business problems with technology", which led to very blank faces and an urgent need to be somewhere else on the part of the person I was talking to.

We rely so heavily on job titles to ascribe value to people in our system, and I had completely bought into that. So, without a job title, who was I? I imagine that this was a little window into what folks who have chosen to care for their family as their primary role feel when they're thrust into a gathering of new people. Our system says that the right label = valuable, and so the first question asked is often some form of "What is your label?" with the intention of using the answer to subconsciously put that person in some kind of value bucket that we hold in our heads. More/less valuable than me or impressive/not impressive, adding value/not adding value.

What do you do when you don't have a label to ascribe your value? In my case, I turned to my productivity as an indicator of my value when I was in between jobs. I started reading business books, I took on more responsibility within our family, I took courses like learning to code in Python, and I got an executive coach to help me work out what I wanted to do next. I would list out all the things that I had accomplished in my day or week and only if that list seemed impressive enough could I feel good about myself.

Manifesting

One good thing that came out of being let go that first time was intentionally spending a good deal of time trying to work out what I wanted out of the next role. At the time, I didn't have any of the language that I do today around setting intentions or manifesting, but what the coach I was working with did for me was to help me understand what I wanted both from a company—their values and the way they do business—and what I wanted from the role, in terms of opportunity, responsibility, and team environment. Together, we focused on going through my career to date, the highs and lows, and understanding what those had in common. The outcome was a clear list of attributes that I could use as I looked for work.

As I went through the process of looking for a new job, I used that list to help identify whether I wanted a role or not, and it proved incredibly helpful. I ended up interviewing for a role in a tech start-up where the environment that they described to me was somewhat of a mess. The good kind of mess though; the kind of mess with opportunity. The type of mess that I could immediately see a way to wrangle. The type of mess that was fully within my wheelhouse. And I was sorely tempted to take that role. I met with some of their senior folks, and we got on well. I could see the role that I could play at the company. But then I went back to the list of things I had identified that I wanted, and disappointingly the role did not line up. As hard as it was, I decided against going any further, even though I didn't have another option at the time.

And out of the space created by saying no to the first opportunity, came a job at a technology company that I'd been following for some time, as I'd worked with several of the founders in my first role in Canada. It matched both the list of things I wanted from a company and what I wanted from my own role almost perfectly, so I said yes.

Self-Sabotage

I've landed the role that matches everything I want, at a company with the same values as mine and the added bonus of being founded by people I like and respect. *I've made it!* Or so you'd think. And this is where I start to try and undo everything for myself.

But first, let me go back a little way. I was introduced to the company by one of the founders, with whom I had worked very closely some years before and remained in contact over the intervening time. The role they were hiring for was vice president (VP) of Engineering, and I'm not an engineer, but he was clear—they weren't looking for someone who could help the department technically at that moment. It was more about relationships, people, and process, and he thought I'd be great.

I met more than ten people in thirteen hours of interviews, including giving a full case study presentation to land the role, and a month later I was in orientation with several other folks starting in different departments. Almost immediately, my calendar exploded with invitations for meetings with all kinds of different people from across the organisation, and I was also spending time every day with the outgoing VP of Engineering to ensure that he downloaded as much as possible to me before he was due to leave, a month later.

That first month was a blur, which was supposed to culminate in a girls' ski trip that had been planned for some time. By the time that ski trip weekend rolled around, I was ready to quit my job. Drinking from the firehose was killing me, and I was held prisoner by my self-limiting belief that I wasn't good enough (specifically in this case because I wasn't an engineer) and I had somehow tricked the hiring team into hiring me. I felt like I was failing already and would never be able to do it. I realize now that I'd decided that success looked like knowing everything that the previous VP knew and being able to do everything he'd done, even though I had been hired specifically because I was different.

We'd had a lot of people drop out of our weekend away, so my friend and I had turned it from a girls' ski trip into one for our two families. And then my daughter got sick, so my husband and son ended up going without us. Left at home, I cried a lot that weekend. My daughter slept most of the time, so I watched a lot of *Grey's Anatomy* and wept cathartically through the sorrow of fictional TV characters. And honestly it was likely thanks to *Grey's Anatomy* that I went back to work on Monday because I was able to release so much of the pent-up tension.

I went back, but I still felt like I was faking it and someone was going to catch me out. I remember an early engineering manager meeting that will forever stay with me. These folks were mostly people who now reported directly to me, and this particular meeting was designed to be a learning meeting where one of them would bring a problem that they were facing and then together the group would look for a solution and see what they learned in the process. Rather than sitting back and observing the group work something through together, I leapt into the conversation with my own opinions and started talking about a book that I'd been reading about complexity theory. I remember feeling desperate to prove to this group that I'd been hired for a reason and that they could learn something from me. It was very much "Look at all the books I've read, aren't I smart?!" <*Shudder*>. In the moment I remember thinking, *I'm doing it! Look at me sharing my knowledge with the group. Now they'll understand why I'm here.*

As I trailed off and the group sat in what was likely stunned silence, one of the more outspoken members said very kindly, "That's all very interesting, Joanne, but I don't see how it relates to the problem we're discussing." And he was right, it didn't. But at the time, I was trying to be a version of leadership that I thought I was supposed to be—the widely read, knowledgeable one—because I thought just being me wouldn't cut it.

In that first year, I offered to resign a couple of times to two different bosses. The Engineering team was going through a tough time when I joined, and it felt like we were consistently slogging uphill. I was keenly aware of the areas where we still had problems and I couldn't bear the idea that the team would suffer because I wasn't up to the job, plus, part of me just wanted an easier life that wasn't as fraught with self-doubt. Both times I brought it up, I was met with reassurances, support, and a flat refusal of my offer.

Despite my inner critic being so loud during that time, I was actually making a difference. When I reached my first anniversary, one of the most senior engineers in the department asked me what I thought I'd achieved in my first year. My mind went blank, but he volunteered, "I can tell you what a difference you've made—now you're here, we no longer leave broken windows," which is to say that I had built a culture of following through and fixing issues when they're identified.

I understand now that the self-sabotage was not only caused by my belief that I wasn't good enough, but it was also the shadow side of my value of personal responsibility. I've always had a deep belief that we need to take responsibility for our actions, but I'd taken that to an extreme level where I felt responsible for absolutely everything. I believed that if I didn't do everything perfectly, then it would be disastrous for everyone concerned. Carrying that burden alone was not only unhealthy for me, but it also meant I wasn't as impactful a leader as I could be. While I was able to make some positive change, I was limiting my impact by not allowing people on my team to use their energy and initiative to address other challenges we faced and so they likely persisted longer than they should.

I'm Not Good Enough

I remember my first career coach telling me at one point that I was an incredibly frustrating individual.

At the time I didn't think anything of it, because it wasn't anything new to me. My husband regularly got frustrated with me at my lack of belief in myself when there was overwhelming evidence to show that I was good at what I did. When I left my first role in Canada, I remember being genuinely surprised by the wonderful feedback I received from folks I'd worked with, who outlined why they loved working with me and the reasons why they were going to miss me. This probably sounds annoyingly modest, like I'm pretending that I don't know I'm good at something so that people will keep telling me that I am. But it's got nothing to do with modesty and everything to do with my strong underlying story that I'm not good enough.

The "not good enough" story started with the good girl identity. Building that identity started with watching and understanding how adults were drawn to me when I was well-behaved as a child, and internalizing that being good was a pathway to being loved and valued. As I grew, I added more components to the identity—a good girl should consider everyone's feelings before her own, she should act selflessly, she shouldn't make anyone uncomfortable, she shouldn't break rules, she should study/work hard and succeed on that basis, she should be clever, she should be an example, she should know how to do things and not make mistakes, she shouldn't have messy feelings, and she should be someone to look up to. With each addition to the good girl description, I added more ways to measure myself against this identity and find myself wanting. More reasons I needed to work harder.

This is the story that I first uncovered when I started going to therapy during my stress leave, but that, looking back, was always there, colouring all of my experiences. And it's a story that served me well in many cases. It drove me on in a way that did lead to greater success. It meant I was often the hardest worker in the room, which got noticed by those more senior than me, who rewarded that hard work with greater responsibility and higher pay. It played well in our hustle culture because it meant I was always chasing more and then getting it, which of course then serves as evidence that reinforces the pathways in your brain that tell you that hustling equals success. Soon you're dealing with an eight-lane highway of a neural pathway, and it's the only way you know to show up.

Adding Kids to the Mix

When I had my son in 2013, our dynamic at home shifted. Going into parenting as two people with full-time jobs who have never had any real commitments outside work, being on maternity leave is a pretty terrible way to set you up for success. You go into it as two individuals who have chosen to be with each other, and share your lives together, and who also have rich separate lives. Then you have one of them stay at home for a year or more (because we have the privilege of living in Canada), and by virtue of being at home all the time for an extended period, that person starts picking up all the slack around the house. In our household that slack had to date been shared, but as I was home all the time, I started to do all the laundry, I'd do the grocery shopping and prep the dinner, I was our social planner, I'd think about where we might go on holiday and organize it, and I was fully responsible for all things baby—learning about all the development stages and what to expect, reading about the best ways to introduce food, ensuring that we had all the supplies we needed, thinking about childcare for when I went back to work, and on and on. Then you come out of maternity leave with one partner used to doing all the things and one used to having all those things magically done. But the *allthethings* partner suddenly now has a full-time job on top of the already full-time job that they were doing.

And then there's our own internal programming. The stories that we've been told, or told ourselves, our whole lives about the way we should behave. Mine says that I *should* be able to do it all. I *should* be able to hold down the big job and be great at it while also being an incredible wife who keeps the household running smoothly and makes it look easy. I *should* be able to be the best mum there is, being present for my kiddo, and researching how I can help him develop, while ensuring that we're staying in touch with all our friends and family.

My husband's programming was built on seeing his mum do all of those things and seeing his dad go to work, then tinker in the garage with no responsibility for parenting or running the house at all. He was already doing more than his dad in showing up for our son as a doting dad who would do anything for him, but it wasn't in his programming to take on a partnership amount of the rest of the work. It's not that he couldn't do it, but that he'd never seen it modelled, so it didn't even occur to him. Add to that my martyr mindset, which meant that I just kept doing all the things and allowing resentment to build, and you've got a ticking time bomb on your hands.

Still, we managed with one kid, and the time bomb didn't go off until we had our second. Then, a couple of months after going back to work again, when our daughter was about nine months old, I reached breaking point, and we had some big fights with me ugly-crying and throwing around the D word (divorce) because I couldn't take it anymore. Having a demanding toddler (which is really every toddler who ever lived) and a baby who wouldn't sleep and going back to work to take on a big project, at the same time as planning my husband's fortieth and organizing a family holiday with my brother, his family, and my mum and dad, led me to snap.

We agreed to go to couples therapy.

While the therapy gave us some great communication tools that we still use today, we didn't dig into the programming that was at the root of the way we were behaving. It wasn't until recently that I was introduced to the concept of "unlearning" things that you internalized as a kid and that cause you to respond in particular ways to particular scenarios.[6] So, while the tools have helped us as a couple, the experience didn't help me understand myself any better—what my triggers are or why I feel the need to do and control everything—so while we patched up our immediate challenges, I went back to doing those things and the pressure began to build again.

---

6   I first heard the term "unlearning" in the diversity, equity, and inclusion training that we did at work. It's the process of identifying mental habits or framing that don't serve or aren't relevant anymore and finding new ones that serve you better.

Masking Up

The pandemic, starting in March 2020, added a whole new layer of complexity to everyone's situation. Offices, schools, and day cares were closed, so suddenly my husband and I were both working from home, and our kids, three and six at the time, were at home with us. We were fortunate to have a nanny, but she was immunocompromised to a degree, which meant that any time one of the kids got any kind of sniffle, it would be two weeks of no childcare while—following the guidance at the time—we waited to see whether any symptoms developed.

One of the aspects of the pandemic that wore the hardest on my relationship with my husband was our different perspectives on what was "safe." If caution and adherence to general Covid-19 guidelines were represented together on a spectrum, our nanny would have been at the extreme end, doing even more to protect herself than the guidelines suggested. I would have been to the right of centre, on the cautious side, and my husband towards the other end of the spectrum, taking a more casual approach in those early days, before we knew how bad it would get and how long it would last.

Our nanny had cause to be concerned about Covid as she was in an age group that had an elevated risk and she had other health issues that could make it very bad for her. As a result, each day she would come to work at our home, wearing two masks, a visor, and gloves, and she would disinfect everything that she might touch during the day.

Before everyone got used to taking masks with them everywhere, my husband would sometimes forget one when he ran out to do something, which caused tension between us, only exacerbated by our nanny spotting him in a coffee shop not wearing a mask on one occasion. This marked the end of any trust she had for him, which then put me in the very awkward situation of having to hear from her all the ways that he was putting us at risk on a regular basis. As a result, she requested that I ask him to stay up in our bedroom during the day (where he had his desk) so that their paths didn't cross. You can imagine how my husband received that. And I get it, but stuck in the middle, as I was, I didn't have a lot of patience for either party. We needed help with the kids, she was great with them and a huge help around the house, and there was no way we were looking for a new nanny when everything was so uncertain. So, we changed our habits, wore masks in the house, and stayed out of her way as much as possible, but the tension remained, with me in the middle.

More than a Manager

The company that I was working at during the pandemic prided itself on being people-first. You weren't treated as a number or a producer of work product, but a full human, with all the complexities that brings with it, and everyone was encouraged to bring their "whole self" to work.

This people-first approach is one of the things that drew me to the company and was well aligned with my personal values. That said, it's a tricky line to walk well, especially when the world is going through such a significant set of events as a global racial awakening, with Black Lives Matter catapulting to the foreground of conversation around the world in response to the murder of George Floyd and Breonna Taylor (and many other instances of anti-Black violence in the US), an uptick in anti-Asian hate, an ongoing global pandemic, clear data demonstrating gender pay inequity, and a new collective awareness of the importance of diversity, equity and inclusion (DEI) in a work setting, all at the same time.

Being a people leader (as we called them) didn't mean just being a higher rung on the communications pyramid in the company. Nor did it just mean that you had people reporting to you and that you directed work for those people. It wasn't like being a manager used to be, when work and home were separate, when private lives were private, and even if you were going through something difficult at home, you were expected to turn up to work as if nothing was happening. Being a people leader meant doing those things that we would expect of a typical manager and also being aware of and in support of the whole humans that were on your team and how they might be impacted by the world, what external factors could be influencing them, and how your own behaviour impacted them, both positively and negatively.

Being a leader of people leaders meant that I needed to do these things for my own team, as well as support them in learning how to support their own teams in this way. I led a team of mainly men, which is not uncommon in engineering departments, and I wanted to help them all become better, more aware, more empathetic leaders for their teams. The longer I was in the role, the more pressure I put on myself to make my position, as a female lead of the Engineering department, count.

I became aware that up to that point, I had just accepted the fact that I worked in a male-dominated industry and had tailored my behaviour and expectations accordingly. I remember being asked by one of the young women in the company how I had handled the inequities of being a woman in tech throughout my career and realizing that I hadn't fought the inequities at all. I'd accepted the rules of the game and obediently played by them. I recalled a time earlier in my career when I'd been unexpectedly handed a 13 per cent raise, not during a regular raise or promotion cycle and not tied to anything that I'd recently done. At the time I was just delighted with the additional income, but now I wonder whether it was related to management realizing how much less I was earning than my male peers.

I recalled going out for a work event with a group of my male peers. It started, as planned, at a restaurant where we all had dinner and a number of drinks. Then all of a sudden, we were piling into taxis and going somewhere else. I asked where we were going, but I was told that it was a surprise and, wanting to be accepted as part of the group, I went along with it. Turns out we were going to a strip club, with me as the only woman in the group. And no matter how uncomfortable it made me, I went in and stayed for a while before making my excuses.

Reflecting on this in my position as leader of the department and watching how the younger women were championing themselves, and speaking out against inequity, I felt like a fraud. I didn't feel any compassion for myself. I didn't reflect on how things were different for women earlier in my career, when it wasn't commonplace to talk about inequity, and being "one of the guys" was the ultimate achievement. That felt like making excuses for my acceptance, and instead I was full of judgement for how complicit I had been. *How could I lead these women when I hadn't fought for these things earlier in my career?*

At the same time, I was leaning into my responsibilities to my wider team, from a DEI perspective. To this end, I was doing my own research into anti-racism and following new people on social media who I felt could give me a better understanding of how people from different racial backgrounds to me experienced the world. I was taking in information from our People and Culture (P&C) team, who ensured that we were aware of anything going on in the media or the external social environment that might impact employees. I was working to become familiar with the cultural differences and lived experiences on the team, and I was only just scratching the surface of all that I needed to unlearn, as a white woman, about how I impacted those around me. So many behaviours and attitudes that I had been socialized to believe were "normal" were, in reality, only normal for the dominant group in our system—cisgendered white people, specifically cisgendered white men.

Two things were true for me—firstly, I loved that our P&C team and our company culture were people-first and specifically, took

DEI seriously, because I believe that if people can bring their whole selves to work, we can be a better and ultimately more successful team. We can contribute more freely if we feel safe to turn up as ourselves. We can build more creative solutions when we have a more diverse set of perspectives. We can better mitigate bias when the individuals working together think differently from each other. And the second thing that was true was that I was completely overwhelmed by fear of getting it wrong.

I would feel the overwhelm, and then immediately berate myself for feeling it, because what right did I have to feel overwhelmed when there are so many living in our system who experience direct racial discrimination on a regular basis.

It was that duality that I found so hard and that contributed to my own stress levels at a time when I was already struggling with what I believed to be my responsibilities to my team, to the work, and to my family, while navigating the pandemic. The duality of wanting to do the work, knowing it was important, and at the same time, being terrified of getting it wrong and then judging myself for how that led to vacillating and inaction. I wanted to keep making positive moves forward and be ready to hold space for learning from my mistakes, and intellectually I understood that this is how to make progress. But the consequences of making mistakes in this space felt enormous—these were human beings I could be inadvertently harming. Plus, the far less palatable reason for my fear was that the personal impact of a mistake in this area could be significant in terms of my own role and reputation. As a result, this aspect of managing my team began to take over the majority of my mental capacity.

I always wanted to do things the *right* way, because I believed there was a right way, which is the safe way and one that keeps everything predictable and calm, but I didn't know what the right way was here. I wanted to immediately know all the things that I needed to know about how my own perspective as a cis white woman coloured my view of situations so that I could identify my blank spots and be a good leader to my whole team. I wanted to naturally view a problem from all perspectives and be able to navigate my team through this change seamlessly. I wanted to do it all perfectly because in the good girl identity I had built, there was no space for making mistakes and hurting people.

Obviously, I was setting myself up for failure and my feelings of shame weren't helping anyone. The work required unlearning so much of what I'd been taught, and it directly challenged the system that I'd lived in my whole life. And that's important and necessary. And it's fucking hard. Expecting that I could do it perfectly made it practically impossible. And then I dug my own hole because I didn't feel that I could admit that it was hard because I've been sitting in this position of privilege my whole life as a cis white woman, growing up and then living and working in Western nations. What resulted was a significant build-up of internal pressure as I both tried to do the work perfectly and simultaneously judged how I was feeling and showing up.

Worst-Case Scenario

I'm never going to forget the sinking feeling I felt when I realized how badly I'd screwed up.

During the pandemic, my company used the opportunity of all of us being remote to expand the areas where we recruited. Up until that moment, we had only hired engineers in Vancouver. We had talked about wanting to become "remote friendly," but we'd all acknowledged that it would be an uphill battle, given that more than 95 per cent of the company would still be co-located in a physical office. Now that everyone was at home and getting used to new remote work habits, it seemed the perfect time to start hiring beyond Vancouver. We started by hiring in the rest of Canada and then we decided to investigate working with partners in other parts of the world.

We did extensive research into the various companies whose model was to hire out their people to different clients for a contract period, which could be anything from a year to many years. One of the key things we were looking for was a company that was a values match for us, that was people-first and that treated its employees well. We found a company in another country that we felt was doing a good job in that space, where its employees could choose which company they contracted for versus being told where they were going to work, where they got paid in line with our principles, and where they received benefits in line with ours.

We knew the announcement of the partnership would cause a reaction, as it was a major pivot from how the company had been run to date. We had always been a company of full-time employees. Understandably, people who were used to that environment, who had maybe chosen the company because of it, were going to, at least, have questions about what this change in direction meant.

I had worked with other leaders to brainstorm what questions we anticipated people asking, and we had prepared a Frequently Asked Questions (FAQ) document to address the ones that we anticipated. Feeling comfortable with our level of due diligence around our choice of partner and our anticipation of the likely questions from the team, we were ready to share the news with the wider Engineering team.

I still don't understand why I chose to do this by posting a short Slack message into the Engineering department channel just before I went into a meeting, meaning that I wasn't around to deal with the response. But that's what I did. I put the announcement in there and linked to the FAQ document and went off to my meeting. I came out an hour later to some messages from concerned folks alerting me to what was going down in the Engineering department channel. It was not pretty.

The biggest reaction wasn't even about the fact that we were going to bring in outsourced contractors to embed in our existing teams. The biggest reaction was related to the fact that I had stated that the principal motivation was to increase the diversity of our teams. My team called bullshit.

One of the engineering managers tried to help with the initial reaction in the Slack channel and offer explanation, but it was evident in the moment that this was not going to help. I needed to address this thoughtfully. And while I recognized this and we set a time for an Ask Me Anything (AMA) meeting a couple of days later, my immediate reaction was to feel personally attacked. Many comments accused me of passing questionable motives off as pure by highlighting diversity. I was appalled that people could think that of me, knowing me as I felt they did. There was a lot of *how could they?* running through my initial response.

The longer I sat with it though, the more I realized they were right; that's what I had done.

I was worried about how people were going to take the news that we were outsourcing, so I played up the side that I thought made the news more palatable. And boy did it backfire.

I didn't sleep that night, or the next, and I spent hours that weekend going over what I might say in the AMA. I didn't want to have to think too much on my feet and potentially make the situation even worse with a careless answer. And if I'm honest, over-prepared is the only way that I felt comfortable going into any situation; that's the perfectionist in me, who is constantly trying to control the outcome by working harder. Growing up, I was applauded for all the traits that are part of being a perfectionist—working extremely hard, always striving to do better, obsessing over the times when you didn't get 100 per cent. It was only when the conversation in the tech industry and in the self-help and parenting domains moved to talk of failing, acknowledging your mistakes, and then learning from them, that I realized the way that I had operated to date wasn't necessarily a healthy way of being, so I used to joke that I was a recovering perfectionist. If I was "recovering", it suggested I was doing something to move away from that way of being, but the bottled fear that drove my perfectionism was still very much in control.

When we got to the AMA, I had one of the respected senior engineers act as the moderator for the event, which was obviously over Zoom as we were mid-pandemic. We had an hour, with some questions submitted ahead of time that I'd prepared answers to, and then space at the end for new questions from those attending. I remember looking at the clock at one point and realizing we were only halfway through—I still had thirty minutes of answering questions to go. I wondered whether I was going to have the stamina to keep giving considered answers and not screw up in some way.

Finally, it was over. I shut off Zoom and sat back in my chair, physically and emotionally exhausted. The response was mixed, which was to be expected. There were some engineers who were happy I'd turned up and answered questions, there were some who had issues with some of the things I'd said, and there were some who were still incensed that we'd made this decision. Managing the situation didn't end with the AMA, but it was the point where I had to draw the line under my own personal screw-up and focus on how best to integrate this new company into ours in a way that worked as well as possible for both sides.

I don't know whether things would have happened differently if I hadn't already been well down the path to burnout. The outsourcing decision made sense for the business, but maybe I would have managed the change better for the people if I hadn't already been on that path. What I do know is that the experience itself contributed to the build-up of tension that resulted in me taking six weeks off from work. It was part of a latticework of my own programming and the unhealthy behaviours that was driving, the environment of the pandemic and all the additional uncertainty and stress that brought, and the circumstance of being in a leadership role while parenting two small children and holding myself to impossible standards across all areas, which woven together became too much.

The Journey Out of Burnout

Stress Leave

My plan going into my time off was that it would be a four-week period in which I would work everything out and come back a different person. Don't laugh! I had seen it happen, so I had evidence that it could be done. A good friend of mine had taken exactly four weeks off work and the person who returned was unrecognizable from the person who'd left. They had their old spark back. They showed up in the best possible ways. They were "them" again. So I knew it could be done. They even told me some of the things that they did during their time off, so I was armed with a plan.

The first thing they said they did was nothing. Literally nothing the first week. I heard that advice as you can tell, because I'm telling you now. I did not, however, heed that advice. I don't recall exactly what I did, but it wasn't nothing. It was probably all the admin that I'd been putting off, as well as planning the gifts and party for my son's birthday, which was only a couple of weeks away, and all the cooking, cleaning, and laundry for my family, because, you know, I had time now. I do remember making all sorts of social plans for the following week to have walks, lunches, etc. with friends and colleagues because that felt like a "healthy" thing to be doing. And

I also remember that I felt worse at the end of that first week than I had the week before I left.

The next week I tried to go the other way and actually do nothing. I cancelled all those social plans and I was going to watch mindless TV and read books, but then one (or at times, both) of my kids ended up with days off school due to being sick, and it really doesn't matter how much of a crisis you're in personally, you're still their mum and the only one who doesn't actually have to be at work, so their care fell to me.

I was worried. I was officially halfway through the time I'd said I would take off and there was no light at the end of the tunnel. Part way through the third week, I met my boss for lunch. I confessed to him that I was really concerned that if I went back at the end of the following week I was just going to slide back into my old habits and this time off would have been for nought. Again, wonderful human that he is, he simply said, "Well you're clearly not ready to come back." And that was it; we agreed we'd chat in another two weeks or so and see how I was doing, but he had no fixed expectation of a deadline for return. And that changed everything for me.

I could stop trying to fit myself into this formula that had worked for the one person I knew that I was using as my standard. I could work out what *I* needed and what would work for *me*. During that time, I tried a combination of therapy, journaling, meditation, exercise, and alone time to start trying to understand the root causes of the constant overwhelm I was feeling that had led to my physical symptoms and ultimately my stress leave. These are the things that wellness professionals tout as being part of well-being. And they're not wrong. When you prioritize time for those practices, they can make a huge difference. The key is finding the right things that work for you, and ideally, finding them while they can be preventative rather than used to dig yourself out of burnout.

Tools

I tried a lot of different tools to support myself on the journey out of burnout, most of which are commonly known, but I've often found that the literature around them is written by folks who have fully bought into and implemented them in a way that felt unattainable to me. Either it required too much time to be practical or it was done so devoutly, with a singular belief that I couldn't channel. Reading about the life-changing impact that something like meditation or journaling had on someone often put me off, rather than encouraged me, because of fear that I'd invest the time and it wouldn't work for me. Hitting the point in burnout where I was concerned for my long-term physical health meant I finally confronted that fear of the tools not working and tried many different things, so I want to share the real-life impact these tools had on me.

Meditation

I had tried meditation, on and off, multiple times and it had never worked for me, but then in 2020 I discovered Dan Harris and his book *Meditation for Fidgety Skeptics*. It's not his first book about meditation, but it's the one that spoke to me because he's a super Type A news anchor who had a very public, on-air meltdown at the peak of his anxiety, and in this book, he takes every argument that I had used as evidence that meditation wasn't for me and knocks them down. I don't think I even made it through the whole book in the end, but the first few chapters felt like they were written for me personally. And that was enough to get me to download his app 10 Percent Happier and start the first of his meditation courses where each meditation was only one to two minutes long and followed an explainer video that set the scene for what you'd be learning.

The first ones that I did were with a meditation teacher called Joseph who was so practical he easily disabused me of the notion that meditation meant emptying my mind and achieving this sense of Zen clarity. He taught me that meditation is more about being present, and that when you identify that your mind has wandered off into something else, you just note "thought" and begin again.

Begin again. It was that simple. Not, judge the living shit out of yourself for having strayed from the path of spiritual enlightenment and then berate yourself back onto that path. Just, begin again. For anyone familiar with meditation, this will not seem like much, but it was a massive shift for me. This path of no self-judgement was not one that I had trodden. The idea that I could stumble, note the stumble, but still be worthy of walking the path, blew my mind. And suddenly I could see how it applied to more than just meditation. How I was making my mistakes so much bigger than they needed to be by reliving the pain and the embarrassment and judging the fact that I'd even made the mistake in the first place. It was really the first time I'd fully internalized that the learning was more important than the mistake.

By the time I took my stress leave, I had been doing the meditations on 10 Percent Happier pretty consistently for a year or so, and I'd outgrown them. They helped me learn how to meditate, which was invaluable, but I was now looking for something to help me understand what I was feeling and get more in touch with my feeling self.

I don't remember who first recommended Sarah Blondin to me, but in the end, practically every coach and mental health professional I've worked with in British Columbia has mentioned her to me. And she was the perfect fit for where I was in that moment. Her meditations assume you understand that you're not trying to empty your mind, etc. and go straight into feeling. Her meditation series is called *Live Awake*, and the title encapsulates exactly what she's helping her listeners to do.

The point here is that you have to find the meditation practice that works for you. As my needs evolved, so the teachers and the teachings had to evolve. As a Type A Fidgety Skeptic, I believe that if I found my meditation practice, then so can you.

Do I still meditate? Well, you might ask. And the answer is, not very often. For a long time, I really needed to, and I needed to do it most days of the week. These days, it is not the tool that I reach for most of the time, but it's in the toolbox when I need it.

Journaling

Like meditation, I've tried journaling multiple times, and it's never stuck until this time. On one of my previous failed attempts, I picked up *The Artist's Way* by Julia Cameron, which talks about "morning pages" where you're supposed to get up every morning and write three pages in your journal without stopping. You can literally write "I don't know what to write" over and over again, but the point is that you don't stop and think, you just write. This is supposed to prime the pump of inspiration, even if you never read the words you write ever again. You're not writing for coherence, or posterity, but to practise getting pen to paper without inhibition.

I tried this because I really wanted to be a writer, even back then. And I couldn't make it happen. I would find that I'd forget to do them, or I'd create a reason that I couldn't fit them in each morning, and this was before we had kids, so I didn't even have that excuse. So, I gave up. I felt at the time that if I couldn't even do this simple exercise daily, then clearly, I wasn't meant to be a writer. I had it in my mind that writers couldn't help but write. Real writers were called by their writing and didn't have to force themselves to do anything; ergo, I was not a writer.

For Christmas the year before my stress leave, my husband had bought me a journal (at my request I believe), a beautiful custom Moleskine notebook. Even though my time off was in September, I hadn't yet written in the thing. I picked it up to see whether things would be different this time.

I had no idea what I was supposed to write, but it wasn't working for me to keep everything bottled up, so I gave it a go. In the end, my journals were a mixture of reporting about what I was up to, something that one of the kids said or did and wonderings about the state of my mental health. In the early days, there were a lot of day-to-day observations on how my body was feeling and whether the physical feelings of anxiety were present or not. There was a lovely realization at one point after a couple of months that I hadn't felt the tightness in my chest for a few days in a row, but threaded through those early entries is a tense waiting for when I'm going to be "better." A clutching at any positive signs, and sometimes a real stomach-dropping despair when I'm having a bad day, snapping at the kids or feeling like I don't know what to do with my body.

I didn't recall feeling like that until I read back through my journal entries at the beginning of this year. As I reflect though, I do have a sense that I always assumed that coming out of burnout would be a moment. It would be a point in time noticeable by a before and an after. Before, I would still be feeling the effects. After, they'd be gone. After, I'd get back to living my life without all the anxiety. I'd be able to cope again with the workload and the life-load, and I'd be back to being everyone's rock. It would be like recovering from a sickness, where once you're better, you marvel at how weak you were and how thankful you are that you're healthy again, until one day, you don't even think about it anymore.

I didn't anticipate that burnout was just the beginning of a new way of being.

When I first went back to work in early November 2021, I used paid time off I had saved up to go just three days a week, then four days a week through to the Christmas holidays, so it was only January when I was back to working full-time. Looking back at my journals from early 2022, I mention quite regularly that I'm not sure how I'm going to keep going with the five-days-a-week rhythm. Even though I was feeling "well", in that I didn't have the crushing anxiety each day, I could sense that a bigger change needed to happen. It didn't feel sustainable to have two parents working full-time jobs, trying to maintain a house, do all the life admin, have social lives, exercise and eat well, plus be present for each other and make the most of the fact that our two young kids actually wanted to spend time with us when they weren't in school.

Reading back through my journal was the first time I could see with clarity that I knew, long before I made the conscious decision, that I wasn't going to work five days a week for someone else ever again. The journal entries themselves aren't writing that I would want to share with anyone else, that's never what they were for, but writing them gave a real energetic release and created space in my brain at the time, and then later, reading them back to myself has helped me identify patterns. Don't get me wrong though, when I heard Tracee Ellis Ross read a portion of her journal to Glennon Doyle on her *We Can Do Hard Things* podcast, I was a little bit jealous that she had written something share-worthy, something that people would exclaim over. Mine are not like that. But writing the difficult stuff, the confusing stuff, somehow declaws it and makes it easier and clearer. Even writing about mundane and banal life events creates space in my brain to allow other creative thoughts to play.

I don't have a daily journaling ritual these days, but I write in it at least a couple of times a week, and more when I'm trying to work things through. I use it for exercises that my coach gives me, when I'm trying to work through a particularly tricky feeling that I don't understand, or when I'm feeling particularly judgy about how I'm showing up in a part of my life. I also use it when the tension in my chest reappears, as it does sometimes. Journaling helps calm the panic that I'm backsliding. It gives me a focus to work through what is underneath the physical feeling.

In previous years, it's taken me a full year to fill one Moleskine notebook, but this year I notice that I'm nearing the end of one and we're not quite halfway through the year at the time of this writing. Likely there's a correlation there between the amount of pump-priming I'm doing with the journaling and the fact that I'm finally putting all of this down on paper.

Exercise

Nobody likes to be told that exercise will really make them feel better, because if you're not already doing it, then it feels enormous to have to start. I've had periods in my life where I've exercised every day and I've had periods where I barely move. What I know is that when I'm exercising, I can't imagine how someone could feel well and not be exercising. And in the periods when I'm less active, I have trouble imagining my way back to that lifestyle.

In the autumn of 2020, a full year before I took my stress leave, I was in a period of regular activity when the pain in my shoulder that had been nagging at me for a while became a fully frozen shoulder. Apparently, this is quite common in women "my age" (which never means something complimentary) and is known as an idiopathic condition because medical science has not worked out what causes it yet. For me, it started with a shoulder "tweak" that just didn't heal. The range of motion just kept getting smaller as the shoulder "froze", with any slight movement beyond the range (which kept changing every day) resulting in a sharp pain that would literally drop me to my knees multiple times a day.

As an active person, who is used to a pretty physical relationship with my young kids—lots of chasing, wrestling, tickling, carrying them, and generally fooling around—this came with quite a significant change to how we interacted. It also meant that I couldn't do my usual exercise, which at that point consisted of lunchtime Zoom workouts with our CEO's executive assistant, who was also a mixed martial artist, personal trainer, and nutritionist. During these workouts, she would find new ways to slightly modify a well-known exercise so that it pushed you even harder than normal and she'd do it all with a Pitbull soundtrack and a giant grin on her face. I loved these workouts. They pushed me, and even though we were confined to our homes because of the pandemic, I was in great shape.

The frozen shoulder brought an end to that for six to nine months. Other than physio exercises, which I was motivated to do for the first time because having only one working arm was a real pain (pun intended), I found that all I could do from an exercise perspective was to hike in the forest. Luckily for me, I live in North Vancouver, and we have ample forest trails for my hiking pleasure. So that was where you'd find me, AirPods in, walking as fast as I could, trying to out-hike the waves of anxiety I was already experiencing.

Sometimes my husband would suggest that he and the kids come with me, and it would only take one look at my reaction to know whether that was a good idea. Sometimes it was fine, but this was also the beginning of me deliberately removing myself from my family because I was giving everything to my work during the week and the only way I knew to recover was to escape everyone and everything at the weekend. The forest became my refuge.

Physical exercise helped me outrun the symptoms of burnout for some time, but we all know by this point in the story that the physical symptoms were just the icing on the cake.

When I returned to work after my time off, a friend introduced me to *The Class*, an online platform combining exercise with whole-body awareness and spirituality. She said it had really helped her anxiety, so I decided to give it a go. The classes I started with were forty-five minutes long and consisted of some cardio, some strengthening (body weight only), some core exercises, and a fair amount of focus on breathing, standing with your hands on your body.

The way I have exercised in my adult life is really the way that I've done everything. When I'm doing it, *I am doing it*. Meaning that if I'm going to exercise, I'm going to get the most out of the time allocated to exercising. I want to be a crimson, sweaty mess at the end with muscles that are screaming at me because then I know that I gave it my all, and most importantly, optimized the time spent. This new exercise modality was not that.

The Class was a whole mindset shift for me, and it took me some time. Initially, once I'd understood that there would be standing still in the middle of the workout and that there would be moments where my heart rate dropped back to regular pace, I tried to amplify the moments of movement so that if we were running on the spot, I was doing high knees to the point of exhaustion, and if we were doing jumping jacks, I was jumping as high and as hard as possible. Essentially trying to bend this new modality to my overachiever will.

Those *Class* teachers are good though. The more I turned up and listened to the words they were saying about moving energy, using breath and sound, which resonated with the messaging coming from my therapist and my coach, the more they got under my skin in the best possible way. I started to enjoy the hands-on-body moments and relished feeling my heart rate climb down through the use of my breath.

I started to *feel* more.

That will sound weird to anyone who is in touch with their body already, but I've lived my whole life from the neck up, thinking my way through every problem, rationalizing every thought, disconnecting myself from my body wisdom in such a way that I was more or less numb, because I'd learned not to trust my own feelings. This is why I went for so long with very obvious physical symptoms of burnout before I did anything about them. I wasn't in the habit of taking cues from my body as to what I needed.

These days I have different ways that I exercise. I work out with *The Class* to get any stuck energy flowing and to feel my body. I walk in the forest to clear my mind and let the creativity flow. I go to spin class for a concentrated blast of cardio that releases endorphins and gives me that euphoric feeling from intense exercise, with the loud music, in the dark, driving my legs to the beat. And I mountain bike to enjoy the forest in a different way, most of the time with friends. So my relationship with exercise has morphed over the past couple of years—from one where it was all about physical fitness, working as hard as I could in the given form, mainly so that I could overindulge with food and drink, to one where exercise was the escape from my anxiety, to a much fuller and more well-rounded experience where I pick and choose what form it takes, depending on what my body and mind need. One thing is for certain though, I need it and I always feel better having moved, even just a little.

Therapy & Coaching

During my stress leave, I had therapy once a week because I needed it, and I was privileged enough to have an extended health benefits programme that allowed me to do it. Then over the following months, I dialled down or up the frequency depending on how I was feeling. Right now, I'm not seeing a therapist because my current career/life coach, who will never claim to be a trained counsellor, offers me enough insight into the areas I'm working on that I feel well supported.

My therapist had an interesting request for me in those early days when we were working together—she asked me to stop doing my gratitude practice. Nightly, I would lie in bed and list the things about my life that I was grateful for because I had read that it helped people feel more positive emotions, improved their health, and could lead to lasting positive changes in the brain. Needless to say, I was very surprised at being asked to stop doing something touted to have such benefits, but she explained that the gratitude practice was giving my mind evidence that I *should* be fine and *should* let my mind stay in control and continue to struggle on. I did as my therapist asked, and it surprisingly did help because it stopped me essentially gaslighting myself and allowed me to accept that things weren't good.

It didn't take long for my therapist to uncover the "not good enough" story that was contributing to so much of my behaviour patterns, rumination, and stress. The approach she took to help me combined cognitive behavioural therapy with eye movement desensitization and reprocessing (EMDR). EMDR is a method that involves moving your eyes in a specific way while you process traumatic memories, so our sessions were a combination of me talking about what was going on for me and us identifying early memories that we could "reprocess" using EMDR.

I very much liked the idea of a practice that was designed to help build new connections in the brain while undoing old programming. It felt practical and pragmatic—two things that appeal to me immensely. So, I went in with enthusiasm and also a heavy dose of *What if this doesn't work for me? What if I'm the one who can't work it out?* This fear meant I wanted details of how it was supposed to work. I wanted my therapist to tell me what *should* be happening when we did EMDR and how I *should* be responding so that I could do it *right*. She gave me none of that because the point was for me to find out for myself what comes up. And the answer to that, for some time, was absolutely nothing.

Those first sessions were an exercise in futility and frustration. I would try to do what she asked, focus on the memory that we had identified and see what came up during the thirty seconds or so of the activity. She'd hit go on the EMDR system and my brain would kick in: *"Aargh, we've started, what's supposed to be happening? OK. Calm down, otherwise nothing will happen. But what if it doesn't happen anyway? Shit! Are we nearly out of time? What am I going to tell her? Oh no, oh no, I've wasted this whole time worrying. I'm failing!"* And time's up. The dreaded question: "Tell me what came up for you" or "How are you feeling now about that thing on a scale of 1–10?" And I would admit that nothing came up or nothing had changed and secretly berate myself for failing at therapy.

Perhaps I wasn't ready for EMDR at that time, or more likely, it was my programming telling me that there was a "right way" to do it and the fear that I wouldn't find that right way was getting in my way. Eventually I relaxed enough for things to start coming up. Sometimes they were sensations in my body, sometimes they were memories, but they started getting me somewhere in terms of understanding this story of not being enough and where it had come from, as well as the behaviours that were inherent in me because of the story. As I went back to work, I noticed that I was able to say no in places where I would have always said yes. I noticed I was ruminating less on my decisions. It didn't completely rewire the "I'm not good enough" story—it still comes up, especially in times of stress—but often I catch it earlier than I would have done, and so it wreaks less havoc than it once did.

I have found a therapist, coaches, and an exercise medium that ground their healing and exploration on the foundation that we are complex beings, made up of many parts, all of which have value, and it's the conflict between those parts, or the resisting of specific parts of ourselves, that causes us pain and suffering.[7] This layering of support that all teach compassionate self-inquiry and the integration of body, mind, and spirit has allowed me to create a scaffold that holds me up, as I turn towards my programming and attempt to undo the beliefs that no longer serve me.

Most of all, I've found that both therapy and coaching have given me a means to see the stories that I'm telling myself for what they are—stories. They give me an outlet to be unapologetically me, warts and all, with no fear of scaring a friend away or shocking them so that they won't like me. Don't get me wrong; I have been lucky enough to find both therapists and coaches that I wish were my friends, and so that fear does lurk in the back of my mind, but I've made the decision that it's so much more important to work through the shit coming up, than it is for my therapist or coach to like me. It allows me to not hold back and to say the things in my head that I wish I didn't think, but the reality is, I do. And you know what? I actually *am* friends with one of my former coaches right now, so I guess that "being your whole self" thing isn't a terrible idea anyway.

Community

As I wrapped up working with one coach, around the time that I took the six weeks off from work, she sent me a gift. It was a slim, paperback book called *The Art of Extreme Self-Care* by Cheryl Richardson. She said that she'd found some of it helpful on her own journey, so she thought I might like it.

When I'm reading non-fiction, I typically like books about leadership, parenting or business. Some of those might be found in the self-help section, but until recently, reading those books felt more purposeful and worthwhile than reading something purely about

---

7   This is based on the work of Dr Richard Schwartz PhD and his Internal Family Systems model of psychotherapy.

self-care. What I'm saying is that it's not a book that I would have picked out for myself, but sometimes others can see what we need better than we can ourselves.

The first page of the book is a checklist, and I do love a checklist! You have to go through and put a check against any of the seventeen statements she listed that resonate with you, and if you check more than five, the author feels that you could benefit from reading the book. Needless to say, I checked way more than five.

The next thing the author suggests is reading the book with other people, and specifically with other people who are at a similar point in life to you. She references accountability as one of the key reasons, which made sense to me—I'm far more likely to do the activities if I know that I'm going to be talking to other people about them at a specific point. But what I ended up with was so much more than accountability buddies.

I went for a forest walk with one of my closest friends around this time. She and her husband were the first people we met when we moved to Vancouver. We were connected through a long string of someone who knew someone who was married to someone, etc., and her husband was the person who picked us up from the airport when we first landed in Vancouver back in 2005. Little did we know that this tenuous connection would grow into such an important friendship. We were already close at this point, having experienced so much together—learning to ski/snowboard, mountain biking, being married to adventurous husbands, having kids, navigating our careers. And we were both in a moment where we were wondering what came next, so she seemed like an obvious person to ask whether she wanted to read the book with me.

I sent her a photo of the checklist and she responded immediately with a "Hell yes!" We then extended the invitation to another close friend, also with a young kid and also on a journey of self-discovery. Without hesitation, she was in.

Our book club started very formally because when I am responsible for something, I go all in. Our first Zoom meeting had a full agenda with time allocations and discussion questions, action items and next steps. We identified which chapters spoke most to each of us and which we were each scared of tackling and assigned leaders for each chapter discussion. The book is designed to be consumed a chapter per month, with an activity suggested that you are to practise for the month, but we decided we needed to meet every two weeks to keep momentum, and we decided to pick and choose which chapters we would start with and which we needed to leave until later because they either didn't speak to us, or they were too daunting.

As the meetings continued, we lost some of the initial formality and created more space for discussion of our lives and sharing what was going on with us, both as part of the activities we were doing with the book and outside of them. Doing it over Zoom, while not as rewarding as being in person, meant we actually did it every two weeks because we didn't have to arrange childcare, and if we only had forty-five minutes, we could talk for a full forty-five minutes, get something out of it, and still do the life things we had to do.

The regularity meant that we didn't have to spend time on the surface stuff as we were more up to date with what was going on in each other's lives than we'd ever been. It meant that we could immediately go deeper if that's what we needed, and it meant that if I took all the airtime this week because of something going on in my life, it wouldn't be long until I could return the favour to the other two.

This cracked open our friendship in a way that I personally couldn't have imagined. Little things that I'd noted and made up (somewhat negative) stories about in the other two were unfurled and understood to be something completely different to what I'd imagined. An example is the way one of my friends maintained a very neutral face when I was telling her something vulnerable, and how she often was slow to respond when I stopped talking. I had decided this was because she was judging negatively what I was saying and was forcibly making her face neutral so that I wouldn't realize, and that the silence meant she was struggling to find something non-negative to say. The truth was that she was working on her active listening—she was trying to hold space for me to unload and practise not jumping in with the first thing in her head but rather giving me the considered response she felt I deserved.

As part of the self-care work that we were doing, we decided to take a weekend away together to the Sunshine Coast, British Columbia. We found the most incredible Airbnb and headed up for two nights of online workshops, exercise, nature walks, healthy and delicious food, hot tubbing, margaritas, and conversations. Oh, and we burned stuff too! We identified things we wanted to leave behind, wrote them on pieces of paper, and set fire to them on a little rocky beach by the ocean. As they burned, we said out loud the thing that we were inviting in to take the space of what we were releasing. I would never have done this kind of thing a few years ago, but the unfolding that was happening meant some of my fear of seeming stupid was also unravelling and I was opening up to trying all kinds of things, held by the safety and support of these incredible women.

It was in that atmosphere of support that we did a workshop on finding your calling. Not "Capital C" Calling, as in the one thing that you were put on this earth to do, but rather, a way of feeling into what you were being called to do now. The workshop itself was wonderful, but what was even more incredible was the time we all spent with the workbooks afterwards, exploring some of the questions and then sitting together and sharing some of what had come up for us. For the first time in my life, the idea of leading something myself, maybe even founding something, came up. And not only did it come up, but I said it out loud. And it was met with "Of course! That makes so much sense!", not doubt and empty words as I had feared.

This community we had built together gave me strength and courage to say and do things that I had not been able to before. I felt and continue to feel woven together with these women. Their community is a big reason I finally mustered the courage to acknowledge the bigger changes that needed to happen in my life, the ones that burnout allowed me to see, including the calling to write this story.

There's Not Enough Time

Something I remember from that weekend away is a feeling of panic that the weekend wasn't long enough. I didn't just start feeling this on the Sunday, when we were on our way home. I felt it as soon as we met up to catch the ferry at the start of the weekend. I remember wrestling with myself at the time because I really wanted to be present and enjoy every moment of the weekend, but a part of me was already dreading it being over.

Time scarcity was a theme that we were all intimately familiar with and talked about a lot that weekend. This feeling that there is just never enough time to do everything, that we're always rushing from one thing to the next, never fully present in the moment because we're thinking ahead to the next thing that needs to be done. Even with the focus that we were all putting on self-care, it often felt like we were "squeezing it in" between all the other responsibilities that we had as working mothers, and feeling guilty for taking the time for ourselves that we could be spending either with our husbands or our kids.

For me, the feeling of time scarcity manifested physically in my body. My chest would tighten, I wouldn't be able to take a full breath, and, in the end, I couldn't fully enjoy whatever, ostensibly recuperative, activity I was doing, because I'd just be worried about going back to my life not feeling restored. As any parent knows (who has the privilege of raising kids in a partnership), when you go away and leave your partner with the children, the moment you are back, you are not only back to doing your "share" of the parenting, but you need to take on more to give your other half a break from doing it all on their own.

My fear was knowing that I wouldn't have fully topped up my capacity reserves in the time away. My husband would expect me to come back refreshed and renewed, ready to dive back into family life. My kids would once again take dominion over my body and time, practically assaulting me with their love and their needs. Work would be more frenetic because of the additional day I'd added to my weekend, so there would be more to do to catch up—fires still burning, waiting for my return.

Even though I was three months "post burnout" at this point and I had been back at work full-time for two months, so I was ostensibly "better", this weekend away highlighted that there was still significant work to do. I was aware at the time that working from a place of scarcity (there's not enough time) rather than abundance (there's always time) was part of a limiting set of beliefs that were going to keep me trapped. I raised it with my therapist, and she helped me understand that this ruminating on the lack of time was dissociative thinking and I needed to identify the part of me that was in distress so that I could tend to its needs. But knowing something is true and being able to do something about it yourself are quite different.

I knew deep down that the years of self-neglect couldn't be "fixed" with a six-week break from work and then back at it, with a couple of additional tools under my belt to deal with the effects. I still needed to address the root cause of my burnout, and the part of me that was in distress about the time scarcity was the part that was sending up the flare to let me know that I wasn't done yet, that something bigger needed to change.

Setting Boundaries

Before I went back to work after stress leave, I spent a lot of time thinking about how to prevent myself from slipping back into my old ways, the ones that had led me to burn out in the first place.

As part of the work I was doing with my therapist to understand my story of "not good enough", I had identified that this belief underpinned a series of specific behaviours that had contributed to the stress and overwhelm I had felt. An example of this was my desperate need to prove my value to everyone, which resulted in me always putting my hand up first if something needed to be done, even if I wasn't the best person to do it and already had a full plate.

I'd also become very accustomed to saying yes to everything without considering what it meant I was saying no to. Typically, it meant I was saying no to time with my family or my friends or a good night's sleep because I was never saying no to something work-related. In my mind, if I said no to something at work, it was evidence that I didn't belong at the level of seniority and responsibility that I'd got to, plus there was a deep fear that I wouldn't be asked again if I didn't show willing, so I'd have reached the top of my career ladder, not able to ascend further.

Being conscious of these behaviours was so new to me that I knew I could fall back into them easily without something to support me. As I love lists, I created two that, if I used them consistently, would ensure that I was making decisions consciously.

One list was about things I would do:
- Focus my attention on the key things I want to change
- Let the little things go
- Ask questions instead of giving opinions first
- Create space for learning
- Be intentional about how I use my time
- Give others space to fail, learn, and grow
- Turn work notifications off at 6 p.m.
- Take care of myself first
- Build reflection time into my calendar
- Move my body every day
- Listen to my body

The other was about things I would not do:
- Say yes to something without thinking about what I will have to say no to
- Offer to do everything
- Get caught in the hamster wheel by not prioritizing my time
- Take everything as my responsibility
- Go to meetings, for FOMO sake, where I'm either optional or where there's no clear agenda
- Compare myself to others
- Work every night
- Check work messages during breakfast/dinner time
- Ignore what my body is telling me

I decided to review the lists at the start of the week, as I planned my time, and then at the end of the week, as I reflected on how the week had gone. I built reflection time into my calendar on a Friday afternoon where I would ask myself specific questions about how well I had done in keeping to my intentions and whether there was anything I wanted to do differently next week. With the reflection time blocked out in my calendar, I found it easy to ensure that I did the activity. The main outcome was that I largely stuck to the things that I said I would and would not do, and if I didn't, it only took me a few days, at most, to realize it and either undo it or at least ensure that I didn't continue in that vein.

This is a practice I still do today, and while the lists don't look exactly the same, the activity of reflecting on each week continues to help me identify ways I'm wasting my time or behaviours that aren't serving me, before they become ingrained. It's also helped me identify the type of work that energizes me and the type that depletes me, which has been extremely helpful as I'm redesigning my work life to create regeneration and nourishment within work rather than just outside it.

Another outcome of this approach is that I've stopped feeling like I don't have enough time. I know now that I used to feel time scarcity because I indiscriminately said yes to anything that people asked of me, putting my own needs last, which often meant they weren't met. The part of me that was so distressed by the time scarcity was the part trying to draw my attention to this habit so that I could change it. Now, when I hear myself start to say, "I didn't do that because I didn't have time.", I immediately reframe it to, "I didn't do that because I didn't make it a priority." If I feel uncomfortable about not having made something a priority, then I know that I made a choice that wasn't in line with my values, and I need to look at why I did that. It holds me accountable for how I spend my time and ensures that I'm conscious of my choices.

Purpose

I had gone into 2022 knowing that I wanted to leave my job before the next autumn planning cycle, but I didn't know what I was going to do. I had an understanding that I needed something with more purpose, something that fulfilled me, that I could talk to my kids about and feel proud of working on when I wasn't with them.

During one of the walks in the forest, while dealing with my frozen shoulder, I had a sudden thought that it was a serious possibility that these forests that are part of the reason we live where we do, that offer us so much of the recreation we enjoy, might not be around for my kids if we continue treating the earth the way that we have been. In that moment, climate change became the thing that I wanted to work on. At the time, I didn't know where to start because there are so many aspects to climate change—climate tech was the obvious place, as I've been in tech my whole career, but even with that starting point, climate tech companies are addressing so many different aspects of the climate emergency, it was overwhelming.

In addition, I had realized that not a lot of the work I had done to that point in my career was generative for me. I had climbed the career ladder, as I was supposed to. I had gained in seniority and responsibility. I was sitting at the senior leadership table, and I was succeeding according to my manager. But so much of what I was doing depleted me. I was good at leading a team, I was good at problem-solving, I worked well with my peers and the people who reported to me, but at the end of each day I was exhausted. I didn't feel energized by any of the work, and I was relying on time away from work, at the weekend, to refill my cup, ready to pour from it again all week.

Two ideas took seed in that moment—I wanted to get into working in climate in some capacity and I wanted to find a new way of working that meant that I could be energized *going into* the weekend with my family, instead of only coming out of it. Knowing this and being OK with not yet knowing how I was going to do it was a testament to how far I'd already come on my recovery journey. And there was still a long way to go.

A Kick in the Butt

One of the things holding me back from making changes was how much I loved the leadership team that I was part of. I had been in leadership positions for a long time, but typically they had been in areas of the business that were somewhat isolated, so I had been a sole leader and hadn't been part of a team for a very long time. In this role, I not only had a great manager, but I also had peers I loved and respected, both for who they were as humans and for the knowledge they possessed in their specific sphere. I was afraid that if I left them, I would never find another team that I liked working with as much as I did them.

As I was wrestling with this, the universe decided to intervene and give me the kick in the butt that I needed. In March, the first of these people resigned and left the business, and then in April four more key resignations happened, with another close friend scheduled to leave in June, essentially decimating my beloved team.

At the time, I recall being surprised by my lack of reaction to the situation. I went into damage control mode, working to ensure that we considered the impact on the teams that these announcements were going to have, rather than thinking about the impact it was having on me. I don't fully understand the root of this behaviour yet, but it's definitely a pattern—I'm quick to accept that something is happening and work out what we need to do as a result. It's a helpful trait at work when a problem arises, as I can quickly move to taking positive action, but it likely has something to do with trying to avoid messy feelings, so it isn't that good for me, personally. In this instance, I don't think I was as upset as I could have been, because it broke the last tie that was holding me in a role that I knew wasn't serving me anymore.

And then it turned out that layoffs were coming. This wasn't a huge surprise as there had already been a string of high-profile layoffs from major tech companies. I was one of the lucky ones, as I'd been laid off before, so when I negotiated my contract, I had negotiated some severance beyond the basic. So, when the news came that I was going to be part of the layoffs, I was ready—and honestly relieved. I saw this for the opportunity that it was—space to unwind properly and identify how I wanted to change, plus build the capacity to take the first steps.

Intentions

The summer of 2022 was when I did my first "contrast to clarity" exercise, taking current things that I don't like or want in my life and turning them into clarity for what I do want. For example, during discussions about the layoffs, I was asked to take on a new team and immediately said no. I understood that in saying no I was likely putting myself on the list of people to be laid off, but I didn't want the opportunity I was being offered, because I didn't think it would be good for me or for the team, even though it could save my job. The clarity I got in the moment was that there was great opportunity in change for me, but this wasn't it.

This was the first step to writing intentions about the kind of life that I could envisage for myself. I started to dream, and write in my journal, about shorter workweeks, great money, work I believed in, work that filled me up rather than depleted me, time with my family, time to myself, being surrounded by inspiring people, being able to follow my curiosity, always learning, and making a positive impact on the climate. It was a long list, but I started to have moments where I could feel such deep-seated belief that I knew I could make it happen. A calm would come over my body, as I imagined living such a life where all those things could be true. I had never experienced such a knowing before.

Then the fear of humiliation would raise its head, and the part of me that felt this the most would start throwing mental obstacles in my path, bringing up evidence of people I knew who had dreamed of something different, gone after it, and failed, asking, *Who are you to think you are worthy of this exceptional life?* That's some deep-seated programming there. Fortunately, I'm also persistent and aware of the programming now. I know that those voices are trying to keep me small and safe, so I'm practising asking, *Why not me?* when they start up. I've persisted with the intention setting and revisiting the intentions on a regular basis, reading over my list, then closing my eyes and embodying the person who can say that all those things are true of their life.

As part of the process of writing this book, I realized that one of the intentions I set was to be able to work two days a week and make enough to contribute my share of the income required to support my family (after we made some reasonable lifestyle adjustments), and that is exactly what I'm doing as I write this. The process works! It's not magic, and it requires a commitment to uncovering the beliefs holding you back then trying to build new ways of thinking and being, which is a lot harder than just doing what you've always done, but the rewards are worth it.

Pattern Recognition

The first thing I did once I got laid off was to decide that I wouldn't try to achieve anything in August but would be available for my kids in whatever way they wanted. They weren't enjoying the summer camps that we had them in as much as I had hoped, so I decided that if they didn't want to go, they didn't have to. And so, they didn't. We spent a lot of time in our yard that month, as we had new friends who had moved into our suite, one of whom was a friend of my daughter's, so the kids had a built-in friend to play with, and we'd bought an above-ground pool that the kids loved.

Posting on LinkedIn about being laid off and my desire to go into the climate space led me to be connected to Terra.do and their Learning for Action course that covers climate science, economics, financial models, potential solutions, and climate justice—a whole range of things to build knowledge in the climate space and help people understand where they might be able to contribute. It's a three-month fellowship with approximately twelve hours of self-study each week, and I started in the second week of August. So much for not doing anything.

My coach pointed out that this is not uncommon behaviour for me. I work to create space for myself, which is what I need, and then

I immediately find some person, cause, or activity that I decide is more important than actually working on myself. I saw the truth in what she was saying and resolved that September would be the month that I allowed myself to sit in the not knowing of what comes next and explore what I might want to do. And then September came, and it was back to school and the kids needed my support, I had my eldest's birthday to plan (the first since Covid restrictions were properly lifted), I was still doing the climate course, I was getting serious about taking on a consulting gig that required some pre-work, and I got involved in helping a friend going through a tough time. And then suddenly it was October, I was starting my contract, and I was no closer to understanding what my "next thing" looked like.

I can think of a few different things that were at play here. First, working out what comes next is hard and scary. There's no "right answer," which as a "good girl" who craves the right answer, or knowing how to do things the right way, is particularly terrifying. Second, the system that I grew up in valued "doing" not "thinking" and specifically a good day or a great employee was one that had evidence of a lot getting done. In my family, we talked about "navel-gazing" in very derogatory tones. The idea that you would sit and think was ridiculous. Taking action and getting things done were the important things, and it's one of the biggest challenges that I've had as I've become more senior in my career. As you get more senior, you need to get more strategic, and to be more strategic, you need to spend more time thinking strategically and less time doing tactical activities, which goes directly against my belief system that value is evidenced by output.

Unhooking from this belief, that my value is in my output, the things I deliver and do for others, is ongoing and challenging because we live in a culture where "What do you do?" and "What did you do today?" are some of the most common questions we are asked. Responding with "I did some thought exercises about the person that I want to be," was difficult to imagine, especially saying it to my husband, who would have been at work all day, and who also grew up with many of the same beliefs as me.

And yet, this is the work, so seeing the pattern was helpful, even if I couldn't immediately break it. I wasn't able to flick a switch and unhook from the desire for external evidence of my value, but I could identify a specific pattern of filling up my days. And the weekly reflection practice helps here because it gives me a scheduled pause to observe my actions and consciously decide whether I want to continue with them or do something different.

Bad Habits

The "I'm not good enough" story, which had quietened over the months since my stress leave, came back to the fore during a part-time consulting contract. I was asked to come in because they needed experience that I had and I'll be honest, I was flattered to be asked because people I really respected were already there.

At this point in the personal work I'd done, I was very clear on what values were important to me in a company, and so I asked about values before agreeing to join. They didn't have stated company values at the time, and some of the ways they described working put up little yellow flags for me, but the lure of a salary, working with brilliant humans on interesting problems, and being able to try out consulting allowed my Warrior Queen mind to overrule my intuition, as she has been so practised at doing my whole life.

Things started off well. I don't like not knowing and I don't like feeling stupid and yet somehow, I've created a career for myself that has involved being the non-specialist in the room, not being responsible for the details but being accountable for getting to the solution, so charged with asking the "stupid" questions. Being new to a role makes those things easier as it grants you additional licence to not know the answer. You're expected to bring fresh eyes and ask questions, and you can sit comfortably in the not knowing as you piece things together.

And that was all good until I started experiencing evidence of our values misalignment. I like things to be very clear and transparent, but priorities changed very quickly and my knowledge of them involved being in the right conversations, which was very hard working only two days a week. Logically, I understood that being part-time was a real reason for not always being up to date with the latest priorities, but it put me off balance and triggered some old stories about not being good enough to be included in the decision-making. And in that mental space, in that fear I was generating, I started acting completely inauthentically. I took on any project mentioned to me, desperate to demonstrate my value in any way possible, even if it fell outside what I was there to do and distracted me from where I could best serve the company.

My two-day-a-week contracting work started to occupy my mind on all the other days that I had allocated to work on my own projects and infiltrated the sacred time with family. I could feel myself turning back into the mum and wife who is only half there—present in body, but not in attention.

After a few weeks of this behaviour, I found the opportunity to talk to the CEO about some of the challenges I was experiencing in terms of lack of information and clear priorities. So, while I had fallen back into the same behaviours and beliefs that had led me to burnout and clearly weren't "fixed," the time that it took me to recognize them and do something about it was dramatically reduced.

While the conversation did clear the air and allow me to go back to focusing on the work when I was doing it and not let it occupy my mind at all other times, it wasn't enough to turn things around completely. When the six-month mark came around, which is what I'd originally committed to, the company chose not to renew my contract.

The first thing I felt when I learned that my contract would not be renewed was relief. I literally felt my body relax as I was receiving the news that I'd only got a couple of weeks left to work. That was before my mind started blaming me for the contract ending, even though I actually wanted it to end but hadn't had the courage to end it myself. At least by then I had learned to notice the reaction my body has before the mind sweeps in and rationalizes or blames, so I could acknowledge the relief and understand that whatever the experience had to teach me had run its course.

The learning turned out to be not at all what I had expected. It taught me that I'm not yet done with the work to unhook from the theme of not being good enough and that I'm prone to relapse when there is a lack of clear expectations. It reinforced that I need to be values aligned in my work, and that means having the difficult conversations with all the relevant people present and being clear in thought and intention. As Brené Brown says, "Clear is kind". It also taught me that I'm still prone to saying yes for the wrong reasons—because it makes me feel valued or because I don't want to disappoint someone, even if the yes means I disappoint myself.

As I wrote all this down, I recognized another pattern in my behaviour that I wasn't aware of before—even when I know that something isn't right for me anymore, I have trouble making a decision to move on from it, and rather I rely on being pushed into the next thing. While I wasn't doing this consciously, it makes sense. There's comfort in the familiar, even if it's not good for me. Staying in a situation that isn't working anymore both allows for the possibility of something different that will be infinitely better, while it also protects from the disappointment that I might not find that other thing. It allows hope and protects from humiliation. The further I go along this journey though, the more evidence I accrue that when I let go of something good, there's something great waiting around the corner.

This consulting engagement taught me, and in many cases retaught me, so many things. And I'm pretty sure that some of these are lessons I haven't fully learned yet, so the universe will keep putting them in front of me until I do.

Never Again

Around this time, I told my husband that I never wanted to work five days a week for someone else ever again.

When I'd gone back to work full-time in January 2022, I had struggled with the five days a week, mainly because I'd realized at this point that the work wasn't filling me up and that the weekend wasn't long enough for me to fill my own cup and also spend time with my family. I'd started to wonder whether it was possible to get to a place where I could work four days a week so that I'd have one day to replenish myself before the weekend, but then over the summer I'd started wondering what it might look like to work even less for someone else and fill more of the "workweek" with work that lit me up.

That part-time contracting assignment gave me my first view of what a week might look like if I had more time to work on my own projects. By the end of the six-month contract, I had written my first kids' book, I had started writing this book and was discussing a new climate-focused podcast with a friend and former colleague. I am not someone who has always had side projects and creative endeavours underway in their spare time, but all of a sudden, I seemed to have not only ideas but also the motivation to follow through on those ideas and the desire to spend time on these other pursuits. At one point, my husband pointed out that my behaviour—opening the laptop again as soon as the kids went to bed—was similar to what I was doing at the height of burnout; however, this time it was because I was excited to keep these projects going and so the impact on me was completely different.

I was gathering data on the benefits of a different way of working. The positive impact it was having on my interactions with my family, and my increased patience for when the kids were pushing my buttons, further fuelled my resolve to get to a place where this kind of balance of work during the week was sustainable.

Writing Again

Writing has been part of my life for as long as I can remember. As a kid I remember vividly writing stories about animals on yellow legal pads at the desk in my bedroom for my own entertainment. In my early twenties I took a journalism course, even though I was an IT consultant, because I wanted to write, and as I mentioned before, I'd also tried *The Artist's Way*. Each time though, for one reason or another, I stopped.

Then in September 2022, a full year after starting my stress leave, I felt called to write about my burnout. It was a genuine "calling" in that I wasn't sure why I needed to do it; I just knew that I did. And so, I wrote my first article on Medium, which I then shared on LinkedIn, that detailed the responsibility I had, the things I had done *to myself*, to get to a place of needing to take stress leave.

The response to sharing the story was really wonderful. People I hadn't spoken to in years messaged me to tell me how they saw themselves in what I had written. They expressed surprise and often feelings of reassurance that "someone like me," that is, someone who seemed to have it together, and who could be relied upon in a crisis, could also experience burnout.

It took me a number of months, but I eventually wrote another piece about what I did during my time off and what I'd learned from it, and that got me thinking that perhaps this could be a book. The original idea of the book was about all the mistakes I'd made in my career and what I'd learned from them, but I realized that I kept coming back to this discussion of burnout. The experience has been so transformative for me that it was the story I really wanted to tell.

I built the courage to tell people that I was writing a book, both because I wanted accountability to stick to it, and because I felt deep down that this was what I needed to do. I wanted the news out there as soon as possible because, in telling other people, I was also confronting the part of me that doubted my ability, as well as my right to do something so bold.

Telling people early goes against a lot of advice about incubating your idea until it's strong enough to withstand the harsh realities of other people's opinions, and my decision is probably a legacy of my long-term programming—I wanted my people to get their reactions over and done with, so I could deal with them and move on. It felt like solid reasoning, but I made it hard for myself because, while I was convinced I was ripping off the band-aid, I was also on heightened alert for any microscopic reaction that might reveal their inner thoughts when I told them. Even though most showed support and encouragement, I often built stories in my mind about the "truth" that they wouldn't speak, which was that they thought it was a bad idea.

Even this far through writing the book, I still have the *who am I to think I can write a book that anyone will want to read?* narrative in the back of my mind. And yet here we are. This is a real case of "feel the fear and do it anyway." It's my continued practice of letting go of the outcome and focusing instead on the action.

The Journey Continues

Family

This is both a personal journey that only I can go on, and it's a journey that has a significant impact on my husband and kids. I am resolved to continue on this path, as I don't believe I have the option not to anymore. I can't unknow the things I now know. Settling back into the old way of being—the safe, familiar way, where my husband and I both work full-time so that we have money, but we're poor in time, connection, capacity, and joy—just isn't tenable.

I know this, and still, I feel immense guilt and fear about how this unbecoming and uncovering is impacting and could impact my family. In the short term, it has meant less money coming in, so we've had to tighten our belts and let the kids know that we can't do specific things. I am working to help them understand that this is the investment phase, where we understand that the lower income is related to my investing time to identify ways of earning money that don't mean a direct exchange of time at my desk for income. I talk about how great it will be that I can earn money while I'm picking them up from school, or we're enjoying ourselves on holiday or reading books at bedtime. I try to think about what I'm showing them in my actions—that I know it's worth investing in my own happiness, that I'm not sacrificing myself for them.

Because the last thing I want them to do when they're older is to sacrifice themselves. As Glennon Doyle says in *Untamed*, "Your job, throughout your entire life, is to disappoint as many people as it takes to avoid disappointing yourself."

For my husband, it's more complicated. He's also got forty-plus years of programming to contend with as he watches me explode my beliefs and way of being. One of the reasons he's with me is because I'm solid and reliable. And then suddenly I'm not, at least not in a way that is familiar to him. He's both extremely proud of me for taking these steps and unsettled at what they could mean for us and for him. He wants to know that we will be provided for in our retirement, and his programming tells him that what I'm doing is a threat to that. And that threat makes everything constrict, becoming an anchor to forward progress. I see the parallels in my parents' relationship and how it was my mum who identified the need for change and my dad who had to respond. Luckily for us, times are different to when my parents went through it. My husband is open to getting his own support to help him work through what this means to him, but it's not easy.

Being part of a family unit, as I go through this phase, is a practice in patience, which is not my strongest trait. I sometimes get frustrated that my husband can't just see what I see in terms of opportunity, or irritated when we have to have the same conversation again, or disappointed when I realize that the original timelines I had in my head for something aren't going to be possible. This is an area where my coach has really helped me to see my husband's questions or reticence as being his contribution to my self-actualization. Needing to bring him along on the journey with me, rather than just forge ahead at the pace that I want, means I've really thought through my decisions. Rather than him being the obstacle, it's me and him against the obstacle.

And then there's the relationship with my parents and what impact this process could have on that. Going through this whole burnout journey, I can now hold two things to be true. I adore my parents; I have a very strong bond with both of them and know that they did the best they could with what they knew at the time, *and* I also know that I became who I am because of my response to their parenting and the environment I grew up in. My brother became a completely different person because of his response. And that's what will happen to my own kids. I've learned from my own experiences, so I'm not going to repeat the exact same patterns (for the most part), but I *am* bringing my whole self to this parenting experience, lowercase t trauma and all, in the same way that my parents did. My kids will have their own responses to the parenting they receive from me and my husband, some of which they'll likely need to undo as they go on their life's journey. And that's OK.

Fear

The grip is back again. That tightness in the chest that I lived with for months before, and that now I know to pay attention to, rather than try to push away. *What does it mean? And why now?* I immediately scan my week trying to figure out what has happened, discounting things as I go down the mental list because they couldn't possibly be the cause. Even after all the learning and unlearning that has happened as part of this journey, my instinctive reaction to the feeling is to try to problem-solve it away. That's my programming again. There's a feeling that I don't like so I need to immediately identify the cause and problem-solve my way out of it, rather than see it for what it is, a natural feeling to have, and a clue to something that will be helpful for me to understand.

As that realization dawns, there's a moment of thinking that I haven't learned anything in all of this. And then I realize (yet again) that this is like meditation. The goal is not to empty the mind of all thought, which is the belief that kept me away from meditation for so long, but rather to notice when the mind wanders and begin again.

I notice the thoughts and the despair that was about to kick in because I'm not "better" and haven't "solved" this. And I start thinking about how to be with the feeling. And that's where I am in my journey at the moment—I still have to use my mind to think about being with the feeling in my body. Even as I attempt to be with the feeling, there's a temptation to use the breath to get *through* the feeling. Breath feels like a good holistic solution that means that I'm evolving and growing, but if I'm using breath to try to get through something so that it will go away, rather than as a tool to sit with what is coming up, then I'm not sure that's as helpful as it could be.

These are the thoughts that pop up as I go through these episodes now. I haven't worked everything out; the original programming is still strong, *and* I'm still making progress.

Support & Structure

In the months that I've been working on taking apart the way I live my life and putting it back together in a form that feels more authentic and closer to my best life, it's been key for me to surround myself with support and structure.

I've recognized that while I need variety and freedom to pursue my curiosity, I also need a semblance of structure or a framework to live in, so I've built my weeks to have a rhythm to them. There are the times when I work to earn money, the times when I work *on* myself, and the times when I work *for* myself. I can be flexible on the latter two (and even to a degree on the first), but courtesy of my reflection practice, I quickly know when I get the proportion of time on each one out of whack.

I've found people to support me in key ways. I still have the community with my two friends from book club, with whom I can be fully myself and confess things that I might be embarrassed to discuss, or fear would make other friends like me a little less. I have mentioned coaching many times in this book, and my relationship with my current coach is one of the most important I've ever had in terms of how she supports me to continue to uncover, turn towards, and compassionately be with all the parts of me. I found a book coach who not only has the experience of writing multiple bestselling books, but who does it through a lens of aligning body, mind, and spirit. And along the whole journey is my husband, who is somewhat afraid of all the changes, and who is still always doing his utmost to support me. I really am blessed.

    I continue to do *The Class* and move my body daily, and while my routine of forest walks gets upset by school holidays and the like, I rarely have a day when I don't close my exercise ring. Because if I don't, I can actually feel the trapped energy in my body, and it very negatively impacts how I show up in everything.

Success

I've been chasing success all my life. At school it was A grades and then A+ grades when they were introduced. It was winning the scholarship or getting the first in my university degree. Then it was getting the job with the big consulting firm and onwards through promotions, pay rises, expanding responsibilities, and a growing team, to the point that I was vice president of Engineering with a team of fifty-plus. OK it wasn't Apple or Google, or a team of hundreds, but it was enough that when I said it, people were impressed, and I felt validated. By the measure of the system I was part of, I was successful.

And yet I was miserable. I wasn't present for my family, I felt wiped out at the end of every workday, and I lived for long weekends and holidays. Was this really success?

I continue to have a dialogue with myself about success and my growing understanding that it's not about status or recognition or salary for me. I'm still tethered to those concepts because I've been striving for them for so long, so it's a work in progress, but with each project I take on I'm endeavouring to understand what success looks like in that particular context. For this book I've thought a lot about how I'll know it's successful. The most obvious measure would be sales and reviews, and that's the first measure that I clung to as I started on this journey. I thought, *It has to be good, because it has to sell, because I need the validation, and we need the money.* But as this process has evolved, I've realized that, while I do still want income from the book, I also want to meet the version of me on the other side of this endeavour. I want to understand where this is going to take me and who I'm going to be. And honestly, I'd like to build community. I'd love for this to be the beginning of something more, where people can come to be supported and feel less alone.

Speaking of different versions of success, I experienced one this year that I had not anticipated, and that was a direct result of the work I've been doing to live more in alignment. Mother's Day 2023 rolled around and my husband told me not to make any plans. I woke to breakfast in bed and handmade cards from my kiddos, then we all went on an outing to Fort Langley, a cute little town nearby. We went around the fort, then had a lovely lunch together, made all the more special by the fact that we hadn't eaten out together in a long time.

When we got back from the outing, it was mid-afternoon and scorching hot, so the kids went in our above-ground pool in the yard, and I got to read my book in the shade. And then it dawned on me—for the first time in years, I had not wanted to be alone on Mother's Day; I had wanted to spend it with my family. To anyone who isn't a mother it might sound awful, to want to spend Mother's Day alone, but ask the mothers you know how much they crave alone time, and you'll see that it's not uncommon. The fact that I didn't want to be alone spoke to a success that had crept up on me—my cup was full enough that I didn't need to ask for alone time to fill it up.

Happy Ending

Did you come this far hoping for a happy ending? A neat wrapping up of all the things I've learned that perhaps you can now apply to your life? Maybe you did. That's typically what personal development books try to offer, that this one will be the one that changes things for you. This will be the pivot point, the book that you can look back on that changed your life.

"Life-changing" is how Brené Brown often described her guests' books on her *Dare to Lead* podcast. And it always left me a little cold because the fear crept in that there's something wrong with me if I hadn't had a book change my life. I've read a lot of books, both fiction and non-fiction, and I've enjoyed a whole host of them and taken lessons from many, but life-changing? I don't know about that.

And also, how can *so many* books change someone's life?

I don't think she's being disingenuous when she says it. Brené (who I don't know personally at all … yet!) seems like someone who just loves to learn. She loves to read books written by folks who have thought deeply about their subject matter. She loves aha moments and she does feel a little changed by all of them. If I put this lens on the books that I've read, then I understand "life-changing" a little better because there are definitely those whose teachings I come back to over and over, that cracked something open in me that didn't immediately close back up again. And potentially it's those cracks that open up possibility.

Perhaps it's similar to the way that your heart can keep expanding to give more love. Pregnant with my daughter, I wondered whether I would have the capacity to love her as much as I already loved my son. And the answer when she arrived was, of course, "Absolutely yes." It's a different love because she's a completely different person to my firstborn, but that love for both of them just keeps expanding and expanding, even as my heart breaks a little with each phase they exit, each "last time" of everything.

There is no neat bow here though. There is no map you can follow that will guarantee that you come out the other side, whatever that means for you. I've never actually liked the books that purported to *have the answer* and wrap everything up neatly because they made the learnings feel less relevant to me. It meant that there was one way to achieve the desired outcome, and if that didn't resonate with me, then where did it leave me? But, if we look at 'life-changing' being an ongoing process of small expansions, rather than a point-in-time moment where everything changes, then we don't need a neat bow because we're not done with the gift inside yet. We don't need someone else's map, because they're not going where we're going.

The Both/And

Today I live in the "both/and" as my wonderful coach calls it. I am more awake than I've ever been. I am more aware of who I am and what makes me tick. I am further along the path to the self and the life that I want to live than I have ever been. I have found an interstitial rhythm in my 'work life' that allows me to follow my creativity and be present for my family, while also paying the bills. I am more in tune with my body than ever (though admittedly that's a low bar). I am more aligned with my zone of genius[8] than ever (I mean I wrote a book!). And I'm still trying to work it all out.

At times, my old way of thinking rears its head and I worry that this self-actualization might not pay off, that I might not get to the financial abundance I'm manifesting. Because don't get me wrong, I want to work fully in alignment *and* I want to earn great money—I have a life and a family to support—so this is no dramatic story of learning some truths about myself and ditching everything on a dime to go live my bliss. Hitting burnout, taking time off, getting into therapy, learning about my

---

8 "Zone of genius" is a term coined by the author Gay Hendricks and refers to a set of activities you are uniquely suited to do, drawing upon your unique gifts and strengths.

internalized programming and then writing it all down in this book is just phase one of the unbecoming—the steps I needed to take to get to the next version of me.

I still have moments of frustration that I haven't worked it out yet—that I still feel anxious, I still snap at my kids, and I still fall back into old habits. But this is forty-plus years of programming that I'm undoing here, while also caring for my family and friends and showing up to take care of my responsibilities. Fortunately, I have surrounded myself with people who, in those moments, remind me how far I've come and how the discomfort I feel when I'm doing something that isn't completely in alignment with my values is because I've uncovered a truth that I can't unknow. While it sometimes feels painful to live awake like this, that pain is there to tell me when I've strayed from my path and how to get back on track.

A wonderful piece of knowledge that my coach gave to me recently is that the brain can only work with the information it has, the experience it has been given. When we look into the future, we can only really extrapolate based on our lived experience. This causes us to overgeneralize, especially the negative things. For example, when I experienced something I didn't like in a consulting engagement, I said to my coach, "'But that's what consulting is like." And she corrected me to say, "That's what this consulting engagement is like." The nuance is important because it means that you can isolate the negative thing, knowing that it has a set shelf life. Applying that to the journey that I'm on, it means that when I feel anxiety or tension arise and I think, *Am I always going to feel like this? I thought all this work was going to make me feel better!* I can remind myself that nothing lasts forever. This feeling is surfacing because a part of me is trying to teach me something.

I don't know whether I'll wake up one day and have a deeply integrated understanding that I was good enough all along. I have seen positive signs recently, in what would previously have been stressful situations, that suggest that it's a possibility. I recall observing myself in the moment with a surprised, *Well look at that, you're not faking it, you believe you've got this!* And I did have it.

What I do know is that while I don't want to climb the traditional career ladder anymore, I'm still ambitious. I want to keep growing, to keep challenging myself and achieving things and being successful in whatever way I define it for each project. And I know I wouldn't change this journey for anything, even in the darker moments. I'm eternally grateful that I had the privilege of hitting bottom at a time in my life when I had the means and the support to stop and spend that initial time tending to my physical and mental health. I'm grateful it happened at a time in history when we understand so much more about our programming than when my mum had her brush with burnout. And I'm grateful that we're at a time in publishing where I can write these words and get my experience into readers' hands through my own means, to help me become the next version of me, and to potentially reach someone else in pain. Sending love.

The Good Girl Community

I envision a Good Girl community where we all support each other while we heal the damage we've suffered as we've tried to be good for so long.

It's a space where we learn and uncover things about ourselves, have aha moments, make steps forward, then fall down, to be picked back up by the community, so that we can keep going. It's not a place where we're trying to show our best selves, but where we're learning to find those selves under all the layers of stories and lies we've been told and have told ourselves.

It's a place we go to ask questions like, *"Why is it always my responsibility?"*, *"What's wrong with me?"*, *"How am I expected to manage all of this?"*, *"Do any of you feel this way* <insert undesirable feeling> *sometimes?"*, or *"Is there any easier way?"*

And in response, we'll be held, we'll learn something new, we'll feel connected, and we'll start to learn that we are enough. We. Are. Enough.

We'll make new friends. We'll hear from experts and people further along the journey than we are, who can shine a light into the darkness ahead, and we'll create.

Imagine what we can do as a community of fully embodied women! We can literally change the world!

Sounds amazing, right?!

Join me in creating this community, for all of us, by scanning the QR code below or visiting www.thegoodgirlisburnedout.com.

Acknowledgements

From reading some acknowledgements sections, it seems that typically family are left until last (maybe save the best 'til last?). But if you, dear reader, only read the beginning of this section, I want to make sure that you are left understanding how important those people are.

My husband Clive believed I could do this before he even read a single word I'd written. He continued to believe when I didn't. That kind of support is rare and to be absolutely cherished. I hit the jackpot with that one.

My mum and dad have been my biggest fans forever and their support for everything I do never wavers. They're private people and reading some of the things I wrote in this book wasn't easy for them, and yet they gave me their blessing. I am one lucky daughter.

My brother's feedback when he read the first draft was so tender and thoughtful it made me feel feelings, which is new for me. Thank you so much, Andy.

This book would not have been possible if it weren't for the wonderful coaches and therapists who have been at my side on this journey, helping me turn compassionately towards myself and start the process of unlearning, which then allowed me to step off the path to my default future and step onto the path to my created future. Specifically, I'd like to thank Heather White, whose wisdom and compassion have held me in some of my weakest moments, Kara Kalin-Zader, who helped me identify the "not good enough" story and Jen Murtagh, who catalyzed this process with her generosity of time, insight and connections.

Pia Edberg, my book coach, came into my life at the perfect time. Her holistic approach to writing books has brought me so much more than knowledge of the book authoring and publishing process. Thank you, Pia.

It really takes a lot of professionals to get a book published and I had the pleasure of working with some wonderful women—Karolina Wudniak on my design and layout, Catherine Turner copyedited the manuscript (any deviations from the style guide are mine and not hers), Jessie Cunniffe audited my blurb and made it a million times better. Zoë Pawlak created the glorious art that adorns the cover and her studio manager, Christina Bowe, made it all happen. I also had some wonderful women read my first draft and provide thoughtful, constructive feedback that led to a much stronger final version. Thank you so much Rebecca Rauscher, Silvia Cameron, Elena Cohen, Mojgan Jelveh, Michelle Bruys, Maridie Rauscher.

Who knew that writing a book was really about building a community?

About the Author

Jo Bolt is many things to many people, and most surprisingly (to herself), now a published author. She's always told stories, but this is the first one that really called her to be told in print, though there will be others, because you can't put the genie back in the bottle. She lives in Vancouver, BC, with her husband and kids.

Made in United States
Troutdale, OR
10/24/2024